DEAD FUNNY

DEAD FUNNY

THE LITTLE BOOK OF IRISH GRAVE HUMOUR

ALLEN FOSTER

Gill & Macmillan

Gill & Macmillan Ltd
Hume Avenue, Park West, Dublin 12
with associated companies throughout the world
www.gillmacmillan.ie

© Allen Foster 2010
978 07171 4831 8

Design and print origination by Carole Lynch
Printed in the UK by JF Print Ltd, Somerset

This book is typeset in HelveticaNeue Condensed 9.5pt on 11.5pt,
and Minion 10pt on 12pt.

The paper used in this book comes from the wood pulp
of managed forests. For every tree felled, at least one
tree is planted, thereby renewing natural resources.

A CIP catalogue record for this book is available
from the British Library.

1 3 5 4 2

Preface

Dead Funny is a collection of curious Irish gravestone inscriptions from across Ireland and further afield. Remarkably many of these unusual epitaphs still exist. While I consulted many of the published books of gravestone inscriptions for graveyards across Ireland two sources were invaluable.

I spent several days trawling through the dozen or so volumes published at the turn of the nineteenth century by the Association for the Preservation of Memorials of the Dead in Ireland. Brian J. Cantwell's *Memorials of the Dead — The Collected Works* (available on CD-ROM from Eneclann.ie) was a rich source of epitaphs from several counties. As a hobby Brian spent years heroically recording epitaphs from graveyards around the country and sets the standard for such endeavours.

If you know of any curious epitaphs not featured in this book, please email them to Irishfacts@eircom.net, or send them to the author c/o Gill & Macmillan, Hume Avenue, Park West, Dublin 12.

Fergal Tobin, Jonathan Williams, Ian Cantwell, Maeve Friel, Michael Slavin, It Hughes, Michael Potterton, Thomas Cosby, Eileen Hewson, Deirdre Rennison Kunz, the kind staff of the National Library of Ireland and the many unsung heroes who have worked to preserve Ireland's gravestone epitaphs deserve credit for their part in this book's creation.

Written in Stone

John Young was Professor of Moral Philosophy at the Belfast Academical Institution in the early decades of the 1800s. The year before he died, "the students of Dr Young presented their teacher with a silk gown, in token of their great esteem and in accepting the gift the Professor said amongst other things 'I have endeavoured to train you so that you may be imbued with an ardent and unalterable love of truth, and it is my dearest wish that this could be written, with justice, on my tomb'".

Little could Professor Young have known that his words would be tempting fate. He died on 29 March and his funeral was accompanied by his students in special mourning gowns and caps of their own design. On his tomb his students had carved their chosen epitaph:

YOUNG !

Moulders here

1829

DUFFY
In loving memory of
My beloved husband and father
GERALD
Died 30th Nov 1989 aged 65 yrs
Also his grandson Kierian
Died 27th March 1991
Aged 16 years
I told you's I was sick

Here lie the remains of Thomas Nichols
Who died in Philadelphia, March 1753.
Had he lived, he would have been buried here.

Robert Russal (1744–71), a stonecutter of Newtownards, Co. Down, carved his own epitaph on a pillar in the local abbey when he was seemingly in perfect health and only 27 years of age — yet he died of natural causes and was buried beside the pillar only a few days later.

Collected by Samuel Palmer in 1869 — somewhere in Ulster:

Erected to the Memory of
JOHN PHILLIPS
Accidentally shot
As a mark of affection by his brother.

CHURCH OF ST FRANCIS, WEXFORD TOWN

Lament him Learning
Science droop thine head,
And tell the World,
That SINGWALL DUGGAN is dead.
Died 22nd September 1826,
Aged 78 years
Requiescat in pace – Amen.

SHANKILL GRAVEYARD, LURGAN, CO. ARMAGH

Margorie McCall,
Lived once, Buried twice

THOMAS TILSON ESQ.
Who cheerfully resigned
This mortal life on
23rd November 1744.

ST PAUL'S, CORK

Repent! Repent!! While you still have time,
Here I lie cut off in my prime,
Tom Taylor,
A Sailor,
Aged 79.

CORK CHURCHYARD

Here lies Pat Steel;
That's very true!
Who was he ! What was he !
What's that to you?
He lies here, because he
Is dead – nothing new.

ST FINBAR'S CATHEDRAL GRAVEYARD, CORK

> Beneath this churchyard stone is buried
> The body of a youth unmarried,
> Death caught him swimming near this place,
> And drowned this hope of human race.

CORKBEG CHURCHYARD, CO. CORK

> Sacred to the Memory of
> Michael Power,
> who died March 12th 1845, aged 19 years.
> may his soul rest in Peace. Amen.
> Erected by his father John Power
> To mark the Burial place of himself and his family.

> O Reader stay and cast an Eye
> Upon this grave wherein I lie.
> Cruel Death has conquered me,
> And in a short time will conquer thee.
> Repent in time make no delay,
> For Christ will call us all away.
> Time is scant; like dew in sun
> Beyond all cure my glass is run

In loving memory
of
Alice E. Sharman
born Valpariso, Chile
3rd Nov 1877.
Died Corofin
25th Sept 1955
Our heart is restless till it
Findeth rest in thee.

Audrey Douglas
born Concepcion, Chile
January 25 1905.
Died Cragmoher, July 20 1968.
Here as ever sleeping sound
Lies our Audrey in the ground
If she wakes as wake she may
There'll be fun on Judgement Day.

LARNE, CO. ANTRIM, ON A HANGED SHEEP STEALER

Here lies the body of
Thomas Kemp
Who lived by wool
And died by hemp.

ST FINBAR'S CATHEDRAL, CORK

Departed this life, October 4th, 1782.
Aetatis 44.

Beneath this stone the dust of BOARDMAN lies,
His precious soul has soar'd above the skies;
With eloquence divine, he preach'd the word
To multitudes, and turn'd them to the lord.
His bright example strengthened what he taught,
And the devils trembled when for Christ he fought.
With truly Christain zeal he nations fired,
And all who knew him mourn'd when he expired.

CLONNATTIN OLD GRAVEYARD, GOREY, CO. WEXFORD

Erected by May Hughes Tubberduff
In memory of her husband
James Hughes, who depd. April 4th 1856 aged 30 years.
In love we lived, in peace we died
I craved his life but God denied.

ST ABBAN'S, ADAMSTOWN, CO. WEXFORD

Erected by John Broder in memory of his
nephew John Murphy late of Camross who depd this live,
Novr 6th 1835, agd 25 yrs.
GOD takes the good
Too good
On earth to stay
And leaves the bad
Too bad
To take away.

KILCAVAN GRAVEYARD, NEAR WELLINGTON BRIDGE, CO.
WEXFORD

Here lies the body of James Larken late of Kilcavan
Who depd this life
May 1806 aged 21 years

Pause Reader Pause upon
these lines here given
On the torturing pains of Hell
and joys of Heaven
One you have to chuse
Therefore take care
what steps you are to take
And how you are to fare.
Therefore prepare for Heaven,
While here below
ensure a long eternity of woe.

ST MICHAEL'S CHURCHYARD, GRAIGUENAMANAGH, CO. KILKENNY

Great king of Glory
Justice, Mercy, Peace.
I vilest sinner of the human race
Thou hast prevented
My request thou hast given
It's of Thy Mercy Infinite
That I am among the livin'.
Glory be to the Father and to the Son
And to the Holy Ghost.
JOHN PASTULL AGED 78 YEARS, 1766.

OLD GRAVEYARD, SHANKILL, CO. KILKENNY

Note the date on this epitaph:

Here lieth
The body of
Mary Cody
She departed
Feb 31st 1782
Aged 51 years

KNOCKBRACK GRAVEYARD, KESH, CO. SLIGO

To the memory of John Kelly
Who departed this life on the
12th Sept 1868 aged 55 years
After a life of labour but
With a mind at ease

Remember man who'er thou art
Not he who acts the greatest part
But they who act the best will be
The happiest men eternally.

CREGG, CO. GALWAY

In loving memory of Rickie Burke, Cluide
Corrandulla who died 17 January 1974 aged
54 yrs RIP. Erected by his wife & family
Rickie like all his clan
Was a great G.A.A. man
His interest in Irish culture was renowned
Men like him don't abound

BELTURBET, CO. CAVAN

**Here lies John Higley
Whose father and mother were drowned
In their passage from America.
Had they both lived they would have been buried here.**

BALLYMASCANLON CHURCHYARD, CO. LOUTH

**SACRED
to the memory of
John McAlester
of Plaster, who departed this
Life the 10th of July 1844
Aged 28 Years.**

**His days dear Boys on earth were few
They pass'd away like morning dew
Take learning by this calling youth
And early seek the God of truth.**

KILMURRY CHURCH, CO. CLARE

**This stone was raised to Sarah Ford,
Not Sarah's virtues to record–
For they're well known to all the town–
No Lord; it was raised to keep her down.**

Thomas Lambert was born in May and died in February of the same year! An inscription on a tomb in County Wexford reads: 'The body of Tho., the son of Tho. Lambert, Gent., who was born may ye 13, 1683, and dyed Feb. ye 9 the same year.'

This puzzling inscription can be easily explained. Before the Calendar Reform Act in 1752, the first month of the year was March, so that in 1683 February was the last month of the year.

CONNEMARA, CO. GALWAY

**This Empty Urn is
Sacred to the Memory
Of John Revere
Who died abroad
In Finistere:
If he had lived
He would have Been
Buried Here.**

Beneath this stone lies Katherine, my wife,
In death my comfort, and my plague through life.
Oh, liberty! but soft, I must not boast;
She'll haunt me else, by jingo, with her ghost.

BALLYMASCANLON CHURCHYARD, CO. LOUTH

In Loving Memory
of our dear son
John W. Kerr
of Mount Avenue, Dundalk
Died 6th March 1950 in his 19th Year.
Happy and smiling always content
Loved and respected wherever he went.
The sun went down while it was yet day.
Thy Will be done

NATHANIEL SNEYD ESQ.,
OB. A.D. 1833
This monument
Has been erected by public subscription
To commemorate a man
Whose heart was the abode
And whose life was a perpetual exemplification
Of moral, social, and domestic virtues.
An affectionate husband,
A sincere, steadfast, and generous friend,
A useful citizen, and a consistent senator.
He fulfilled the various duties of his station in society
With exemplary fidelity and unsullied honour
Impressed with a sense of unaffected piety
And animated by a spirit
Of the purest and most diffusive benevolence
And ever found his own happiness in promoting the
Happiness of others.
Such was the genuine goodness of his nature
And such the instinctive urbanity of his deportment
That during a life passed in varied
And extended intercourse with the world,
He was never known to alienate a friend,
Or to create even in times of great political exasperation
A personal enemy.
Inscrutable are the dispensations of providence.
This man so blameless in all the relations of being,
So respected and so beloved,
Perished by the hand of violence.
But it was the indiscriminating violence of an
Unhappy maniac.

While the universal sentiment of profound and poignant
sorrow excited by the afflicting event
Amongst all classes of his fellow citizens
Supplied the truest and the most expressive tribute
To those virtues
Of which it is the purpose of this memorial
To preserve the record
And
To perpetuate the remembrance.

DEANSGRANGE CEMETERY, CO. DUBLIN

In loving memory
Of
Mary Edith Coleman
Who died at Blackrock
On Sept 23 1906
For her devoted care of the wounded soldiers
Both French and German
In the Franco-Prussian War
In the year 1870
Under the auspices
Of the Red Cross Society
She was as Mrs Alsager
Decorated by the Emperor William
With the Order of the Iron Cross.

Sacred to the memory of
Mr Fredr Barker, stone cutter, late of this parish,
who died 21st of March aged 58 years.
His son Thomas died the 28th of August 1783
aged 9 months.
His eldest son Fredr was killed by the French
at Rugheda in Spain
Dec 13th 1808 aged 27 years.
Here also lie the remains of Mrs Elizabeth Barker,
widow of the above Fredr Barker, who departed this life
Feby 20th 1811
aged 64 years.

ST JOHN THE BAPTIST CHURCHYARD, CASTLE AVENUE,
CLONTARF, DUBLIN 3

DOCTOR WILLIAM FAUSETT T.C.D., M.R.C.S.I.
Movile, died Novr 29th, 1880, aged 69
Years, for 43 years the beloved physician
Of Clontarf

Parents and Siblings

ST MOLUA'S CHURCH, DRUMSNATT, CO. MONAGHAN

In memory of two loving and loved sisters,
Emily Wilde aged 24 and Mary Wilde, aged 22,
who lost their lives by accident in this parish,
Nov 10th 1871.
They were lovely and pleasant in their lives and in death
they were not divided
(II Samuel Chap 1, v 23).

These were Oscar Wilde's sisters who had grown up
with Sir William Wilde's brother, who pretended to
be their father.

ATHLONE ABBEY, CO. WESTMEATH

John Tobin
Died 11 December 1848 aged 15
Those who dryst. the mourners tears
How dark the world would be
If when deceived and wounded
We could not fly to Thee.
Erected by his brother James.

Erected by Mary Ennis In Memory of her beloved Parents James & Rose Ennis also her Brother Thomas and her sister Mrs Anne Connor

Worn out with Sickness and Disease
One Lieth Here to Take His ease
A Faithful Friend a Husband Dear
A Loving Father Lieth Here.

Erected by Mrs. Mary Christy, California,
In memory of her beloved Father Hugh Carroll,
Stabannon, who departed this life, November 20th, 1869,
aged 74.
Her brother Patrick Carroll, who died Nov. 5th, 1847,
aged 21, also
Her brother James Carroll, who died Sep. 10th, 1839,
aged 16 years.

In the far West I now sojourn,
Where the Pacific bathes the golden shore,
Thoughts of old Ireland make me mourn;
Where they now lie I'll never see more.

OLD CHURCH OF THE HOLY TRINITY, CORK

**Gods – Pace
Be – Wi – You – My
Tow – Goo – Shisters
Ellenor and Margaret
1673**

KILDROUGHT GRAVEYARD, CELBRIDGE, CO. KILDARE

**William Annesley Aged 63 lyes here,
With him Hezekiah, Thos, and Elizabeth Dear,
His children three, by Isaac his kind son,
Their loveing Brother this Tombstone was Done,
To shew their graves ye same he this Did Make,
Till God's Loud Trumpet Shall bid ye dead awake.**

KILLYLEAGH GRAVEYARD, CO. DOWN

**Erected by James Maguire of New York,
Late of Killyleagh, in memory of his beloved brothers
Edward & Hugh
Who died of fever in the month of July 1845,
Edward Æ 20 years and Hugh Æ 18 years.
Our days are as the grass or like the morning flower
If one sharp blast sweep o'er the field, it withers
in an hour.
Also the remains of their father Philip Maguire**

DONAGHADEE GRAVEYARD, CO. DOWN

Erected by Ann Boyd in memory of her mother Ann Boyd
who departed this life Jany. 25th 1841 aged 64 years.
Afflictions sore, long time have I bore
Physicians all in vain
Till God did say when he did please
And ease me of my pain.

Happy soul, she's free from harm
She's sheltered in her Saviour's arms.

FAITHLEGG GRAVEYARD, CO. WATERFORD

In loving memory of Martha A. Murphy, Trerise, Cheekpoint,
Who died 11th Feb 1971 aged 90.
Her sister Ellen A. Hanlon died 1st April 1944 aged 71.
My memories of you
Will never grow old
They are locked in my heart
In letters of gold
Death cannot part or
Distance divide
For each day of my life
You walk by my side.

HOLY CROSS CHURCH, KILLEA, DUNMORE EAST,
CO. WATERFORD

**In loving memory of
James Higginbotham
died 19th April 1927.
Sleep on dearest father
Thou art blest
We miss you much
But God knows best.
Safe in the shelter of the Sacred Heart.**

DONAGHADEE GRAVEYARD, CO. DOWN

**Erected by David McGrattan of Newtownards
in memory of his honoured mother
Sarah McGrattan alias PURVIS
Who departed this life on the 13th day of June
A.D. 1855 aged 65 years
I'm kneeling by your grave, mother
The last of all the seven
The youngest that we loved the best
Last night returned to heaven.**

DONAGHADEE GRAVEYARD, CO. DOWN

Erected by Rebekah LYONS of D.dee
In memory of her mother Janet McHary
alias BROWN who died Novr. 17th 1829 aged 52 years.
Also the said Rebekah Lyons who died 25th Decr. 1870
aged 68 years.
Tender friends a while may mourn
Me from their embrace torn.
Dearer, better friends I have
In the realms beyond the grave.

ST PATRICK'S GRAVEYARD, DOWNPATRICK, CO. DOWN

I.H.S.
Erected by Thomas Ryan,
In loving memory of his father Thomas D. Ryan
Who departed this life 1st Oct. 1894 aged 76 years
Lord now the time returns
For wearied man to rest
And lay aside those pains and cares
Of which he is oppressed.
Praise ye the Lord. Alleluia
R.I.P.

The dew drop that falls tho' in silence it rolls,
Shall long keep her memory green in our souls.
Beneath this stone are shrouded the remains of Dorothy,
wife of James
Greer who died the 30th day of October 1823 aged 54 years.
To perpetuate the remembrance of her fidelity and
attachment to her husband, her arduous love and
affectionate tenderness to her children this stone was
erected by her son Henry Greer.

ST AUDOEN'S CHURCH, HIGH STREET, DUBLIN 8

This stone was erected to the memory of William
Doolittle, of Bridge Street, in the city of Dublin,
Merchant, and his sister, Elizabeth Doolittle,
otherwise Slator,
Who departed this life the 14th August 1796,
Both aged 48 years. Who, whilst they lived, loved and
Feared God, and was affectionate and kind to each other,
Well loved and respected by all their acquaintance,
And happy are they who are in such a state prepared
At all times to meet their God. Here also lieth 4 of
Their children.

Children

**HERE LYETH THE BODYE.OF.
THOMAS.THE.SONNE.OF.ARNOLDE
WINEKLE WHO DYED THE 11°
DAY OF NOVEMBER ANNO DNI 1697
I lived till deathe did soule & body sever
On earth a while to live in heaven for ever**

**Sacred to the memory of
John McDonnell who Depd ys
Life the 22 Febr 1828 agd 9 yrs
Short was my time long will be my rest
God took me when he thought best
To grieve for me alas it is vain
We only part to meet in heaven again
Ercd by his father Wm McDonnell
And his mother Mary McDonnell
Alias Connor
May they rest in peace
Amen.**

To The Memory of Ann Flin
A friend that loved thy earthly form when here,
Erects this stone to dust he held most dear;
Thy happy genius oft his soul reviv'd,
Nor sorrow felt he till of thee depriv'd:
Peace to thy gentle shade, and endless rest
To they fair soul, now numbered with the blest!
Yet take these tears — mortality's relief,
And, till I share thy joy, forgive my grief:
These little rites — a stone, a verse — receive,
'Tis all a father, all a friend can give.

Deceased September 18, 1766,
Aged near 21 years.

Her father Lawrence Flin erected these touching words.

ST MOGUE'S, FETHARD-ON-SEA, CO. WEXFORD

This dreary region contains Charles only beloved child
of Harriett Dixon.
His gentle spirit left the arms of his Earthly advocate
for the bosom
of his Heavenly one on 6th of March, 1815, aged 15 years
Dear Boy within this stone
The mother's hopes receive their doom.

OLD CATHEDRAL, ARDMORE, CO. WATERFORD

**In memory of
Anna the infant daughter of
Patrick and Anna Carolina Smith
Who died April 9th 1834.**

**Oh! Sweet my baby liest thou here
So low, So cold and forsaken
And cannot a fond mother's tear
Thy once too lovely smile awaken
Ah! Now within this silent tomb
A mother's hopes received their doom
Ah! I shall ne'er forget the kiss
I gave thee on that morn of mourning
The placid cheek bespoke the bliss
Of innocence to God returning
May'st thou return that kiss to me
In realms of bright eternity.**

ST PAUL'S, BRAY, CO. WICKLOW

**This stone is erected here by Lettice
Saunders in memory of her Daughter
Mary Saunders who departed this life
The 3d. Day of April 1807
Aged 13 years.**

**The grass is green the rose is red
Here lies my name now I am dead.
Mary Saunders.**

**Under this stone lie two babies dear,
One is buried in Connaught, and the other here.**

ST MICHAEL'S CHURCH, CASTLEPOLLARD, CO. WESTMEATH

**Near this spot lies interred Miss Catherine Gunning
eldest daughter to Barnaby Gunning of Hollywell in
The county of Roscommon esqr and of
Mrs Anne Gunning alias
Staunton. Good nature and sweet disposition as well as
Beauty were the ornaments of her infant years.
These were soon Joynd by Judgement and discretion.
Religion and patience adorning her many virtues conducted
her to a blissful state of Immortality from her
afflicted Parents
and sorrowful friends in the Nineteenth year of her
age on the
fifteenth day of November 1752.**

**Here underlies too sad a truth
Discretion, innocence & youth
Death veil thy face, thy cruel dart
Has virtue pierced to Beauty's heart**

Sacred to the Memory
Of
Henry Seymour
Son of Henry and Lucie Moore.
Who was born July 6 1819
And called to his heavenly home, May 8th 1823.
His mortal remains rest by the
Side of his sister whom he tenderly loved
And their angel spirits before the throne of
God sing together their Redeemer's praise.

ATHLONE ABBEY, CO. WESTMEATH

To the memory
Of three interesting children
Maria Elleanor and Daniel by
Their father James Murray AD 1820
Destined to bliss behold
Were left a world of strife
And with God and Saints of old
Enjoy eternal life
And young and free of crime
When death his arrows threw
The heavenly mandate came
Midst Seraphim we flew
Then farewell children dear
Thy lives we strove to save
Hope sooths the parents grief
Who looks beyond the grave.

ST NICHOLAS COLLEGIATE CHURCH, GALWAY

HERE · LYETH · THE
BODY · OF · ELIZA
BETH · KINGCORNE · WHO
DIED · THE · 10 · OF NOVBER
1684
THE · SHORTEST · LIFE
THE · LONGEST · REST
GOD · TAKS · THEM · SOVNEST
WHOM · HE · LOVETH · BEST

ASKEATON, CO. LIMERICK

In Memory of Catherine only child and heiress of Thomas
Spring of Ballycrispin, Co. Kerry, married to Stephen E. Rice
X AUG. MDCCLXXXV died May 20 MDCCCXX
and to his dear wife
And Dutiful Son Awfully removed from this World within one
Fortnight and buried on same day.
This Monument is erected
By the unhappy and surviving father.

ST MARY'S, ATHLONE, CO. WESTMEATH

Here Lyeth a virgin of unspotted fame,
Daughter of Joseph Sproule & Joice by name,
Hither let pious maidens oft repair
And as they pass lett fall a Silent tear.
Obit 22d dic Augst Ann Dom 1726
Et Aetatis Sue 19e.

ST NICHOLAS COLLEGIATE CHURCH, GALWAY

Sacred
To the memory of
Wm Page who departd
This life February 6th 1817
Aged 12 years
He was Only Son of
Quarter Master
Wm Page 12 Regt of foot

Cut off in early years a youth
Of Beauty innocent faith
His Fathers hope his Mothers Joy
Sweet William was a charming boy
Obedient to his Makers call
He left his Parents, sisters all
His soul in heaven with Angels roam
His body here beneath this stone

Sacred to the memory of
JAMES JOHNSTON KEARNEY
Who departed this life 22nd of February 1837
Aged 11 years.
This monument is Erected by his afflicted Mother who
Altho' Sorrowing not as one without hope for her
Beloved Child trusting in the atonement of a crucified Jesus
Resigned this life in peace she trusts she acquiesces to his
Blessed will who had desired her not to forbid little Children
To come unto him for that of such is the Kingdom of Heaven
St. Mathw 19th Chap. 14 Verse.

His death was occasioned by his Top having fallen
From him and stopping to regain it a Car rolled
On him in the street.

Fairest flower of nature's Garden blessed.
Permitted just to bloom to bud but plucked in haste.
Angels beheld him ripe for future joys to come.
And called by God's command a Brother home.

CASTLETOWN GRAVEYARD, DUNDALK, CO. LOUTH

IHS
Gloria in Excelsis Deo
This stone was erected by
Patrick Connolly of Tavnaghmore A.D. 1809
For his son James who died 10th Feby 1806 aged 14 years.

Youth like the spring will soon be past
And in the grave will be laid at last.

CABBAGE GARDEN, KEVIN STREET LOWER, DUBLIN 8

This stone was erected by William Dycear in memory
Of his beloved daughter, Mary Dycear who departed
This life June 19th 1814 aged 17 years.
The voyage of life's end,
The mortal affliction is past,
The age that in heaven she'll spend,
Forever and ever shall last.

RATHFARNHAM CHURCHYARD, CO. DUBLIN

**This stone belongeth to John Creathon of Patrick Street
and his posterity
Here lieth many of his children
And tho here they lie in putrid state,
Reader think surely will be your fate,
And whist you have that power that's given to man,
Pray merit a seat in heaven**

ST MUNCHIN'S GRAVEYARD, LIMERICK CITY

**Here Elinor Younge her body,
Lies of whom tis truly said she
Aither a virgin lived
And ere deceast a maiden
The daughter of Thomas and Mary
Younge 26th Feb, 1649.**

DRUM LANE ABBEY CHURCH, CO. CAVAN

**Susannah Brooke entombed here,
Who died of age ye 13 year,
Xber the years 30 and three,
17 hundred added must be,
When ye virgin departed lamented by all
and heavenly promotion was her earthly fall.**

Beneath this stone are deposited the mortal remains of
two young friends,
Master Walter Young of Monaghan & Alexander
Crossle of Anahoe House,
County Tyrone. They were playmates in infancy who, having
being separated by the contingencies of life, are now met at
a distance from their native homes, to part no more. The
former departed this life on the 22nd September 1824 aged
13 years, the latter on the 14th February 1825 in the 12th
year of his age.

KILL ST LAWRENCE, CO. WATERFORD

Underneath her interred lies 4 of the children of Val Kelly of
Waterford City, Gent.
The shades of death escape none can.
Namely John, Val, Honr & Anti departed this life in infancys.
Dated 24th November 1751.

KILL ST LAWRENCE, CO. WATERFORD

IHS
Erected by Thomas Nevill in memory
Of his son and dater Ellen and John Nevill
Departed May the 14 1831 aged 22 years.
I pray good people as you pass by
Pray for us here we lie.

KILL ST LAWRENCE, CO. WATERFORD

I need no pity
No sin I knew
Parents Death called me
To intercede with God for you.
Francis Scully agd 3 yrs. 1834
Michael Scully fecit.

CROOK, GAULTIER, CO. WATERFORD

Here lies the body of Dorothea Wallis
who dyed February 6th 1812 in her 14th year.
She was an angel on earth; we hope and trust in God she is
an angel in heaven.

Couples

Dates from the 1600s.

> Love and age have joynd in one
> To lay the[ese] two under this stone
> Sir Tho[mas] Ash and his Lady Elizabeth
> [unite their] ashes in this house of death
> [and n]ow both having run their glasses
> [they hop]e to be reviv'd from ashes.

CABBAGE GARDEN, KEVIN STREET LOWER, DUBLIN 8

> Underneath Lyeth the remains of Mr John Lyons who
> Departed this life February 7, in the 37th year of his
> Age. 1798.
> Here also lieth his much lamented friend Miss Annie
> Major who departed this life in the 17th year of her
> Age the 15th day of October 1784.
>
> It was not age that tottered to this grave,
> But blooming & in youthful prime,
> Here dropped the beauty nature gave,
> And here will slumber to the end of time.

ST NICHOLAS COLLEGIATE CHURCH, GALWAY

M
A:C

Abraham Marsh
All and Celia

GRANGEBEG, TEMPLEBOY, CO. SLIGO

Here lie Tom and his wife Mary,
His surname Burne, hers was Farry.
She modest was, to strangers good.
He Greek and Latin understood.
As they shar'd freely what was giv'n
Pray that their souls may rest in Heav'n.

CASTLEBAR, CO. MAYO

To these, whom death again did wed
This grave's the second marriage bed;
For though the hand of fate could force
'Twixt soul and body a divorce,
It would not sever man and wife
Because they both lived but one life.
Peace, good reader, do not weep;
Peace, the lovers are asleep;
They, sweet turtles! folded lie
In the last know that love could tie;
Let them sleep, let them sleep on
Till this stormy night be gone
And the eternal morrow dawn;
Then the curtains will be drawn
And they wake into a light
Whose day shall never die in night.

BALLYHUSKARD OLD GRAVEYARD, CO. WEXFORD

Erected by Laurence Redmond in memory
Of his father Patrick Redmond & mother
Margaret Als Sinnott Depd This
Life Jan 19th, 1819
He aged 79 & She 72 Yrs.
Married we were upon a day and departed upon another.
Buried we were in Native Clay in both one day together.
Fifty years and two we lived in Marriage State
Reader Pray for you Must share death's certain Fate.

GOWRAN, CO. KILKENNY

Here lieth the bodies of Mr. James Keally, sometime of the towne of
Gawran, Gentleman, who died Ano Dni 16 [ ] and of Mrs. Ellen Nashe
His first wife who died the 30 day of the moneth of July Ano Dmi 1640
And of Mrs Mary White his second wife who died the [ ] day of the
Moneth of [ ] Ano Dmi 16 [ ]. He erected this monument for himselfe,
His wivfes and children in the moneth of December Ano Dmi 1646.

Both Wivfes at once alive he could not have:
Both to injoy at once he made this grave.

ST ANDREW'S, SUFFOLK STREET, DUBLIN 2

Here lies the
Body of
Charles Henry Meares Esqre
Of the City of Dublin
Born 2nd August 1769 died 4th April 1884
Also the remains of
Frances Maria his wife who
With several of their children
Have long since mingled with
Their native earth

Donald Macdonagh and his wife Maria O'Conor
Caused this monument to be made for themselves and
their posterity,
On both sides, A.D. 1685
Remember Death.
A fine form, the good will of the people, youthful ardour
And wealth have snatched from thee how to know
what man is.
After the man, a worm, after the worm foul smell
and horror.
Thus even man is turned into what is not a man.
Thus the glory of this world passes away.
Whoever thou art who shall pass by
Pause, read carefully, and lament.
I am what thou wilt be, and have been what thou art,
Pray for me, I beseech thee.

In loving memory
Of
Randal Stephen
Lanigan O'Keefe
(Tara)
Died 1st Jan 1990
Aged 80 years
'Gone Fishing'

His Beloved Wife
Eileen Amena (Dan)
Died 7th May 1990
Aged 77 years
'Gone Away'

Just one prayer

This couple loved hunting and fishing. A fox and a fish are carved on the headstone.

Husbands

TEMPLECORRAN GRAVEYARD, CO. ANTRIM

A filial son, a husband true and kind
A calm adviser & instant friend
By justice guided wealth he sought to find
That wealth when found he usefully might spread
Since he loved to teach & to receive
Excels he shun'd but sought the social ring
Worth he prized in beggar or in slave
And spurn'd deceit tho in a priest or king
He strove for truth when truth he thought he scann'd
He branded error while he felt her rod
Yet by kind acts he reverenced his God
Here lies William Logan, died 16th April 1797 aged 29 years

DUNMORE EAST, CO. WATERFORD

Sacred to the memory of
John Wilson who depd
This life 28th December 1847 aged 70 years.
The winter of trouble is past
The storms of affliction are o'er
The struggle is ended at last
And sorrow and death are no more
This tribute is erected by his affection widow.

A light is from our household gone
a voice we loved is stilled
a place is vacant in our house
which never can be filled
Erected by Jane Grabbe,
in loving memory of her husband Thomas Grabbe,
who died 8th February 1897, aged 64 years.

Cease my young beloved wife
To sigh above my tomb;
We yet shall meet in land divine
Where death can never come.
Prepare to follow me and join
My sure eternal home
Erected by Margaret Arthurs
for her husband Hugh Mecagherty
who died aged 26 1839.

KILNENOR, CO. WEXFORD

Erected by
Johanna Synnott of Ustodam
In memory of her beloved husband
Thomas Synnott
Who died 18th Janry 1860 aged 75 years
Also his father & mother & brother Patrick
Who was interred here from time to time.

THE CORD CEMETERY, DROGHEDA, CO. LOUTH

Beneath This Stone there lyeth One
That still his Friends did please
To Heaven I hope hes surely gone
To Enjoy Eternal Ease

Here lyeth the body of John Dowdall who departed this life
The 16th Day of October 1778 in the 29th year of his age.
Of your charity pray for the soul of Anne wife of
Arthur Quinn
Who died 5th April 1879 in her 74th year.
And of Arthur Quinn who died 4th May 1886 in his 80th year.
Both of them died at Liverpool and were interred here.

Peter Drelincourt Died 1720

Such was the second Drelincourt, a name
Victorious over Death and dear to Fame;
The Christian's praise, by different measures won,
Successive grace the father and the son.
To sacred service one his wealth consigned,
And one the living treasure of his mind;
'Twere rash to say whose talent did excel.
Each was so rich, and each improved so well,
Nor was his charity delayed till death,
He chose to give what others but bequeath.
Much though he gave and oft, yet more he meant,
Had life proportioned to his will been lent.
But to complete a scheme so well designed.
Belongs to her who shared his bed and mind,
Whose pious sorrows thus to future days
Transmit his image and extend his praise.

I.H.S.
Erected by Catherine McDonnell of Drogheda
In memory of her beloved husband James McDonnell
Who departed this life 17th July 1832 in the 54th year
Of his age and two of his children who died young.
Also the remains of Elizabeth mother to James who
departed this life 16th January 1828 in the 83rd year
of her age. Also his father Hugh who died 24th February
1829 in the 76th year of his age.

EPITAPH OF JAMES McDONNELL
Written by his daughter Eliza

Join me in grief all you that do pass by
And view the spot where my father lies
Most cruel death, that surely conquers all
Extinguished life and caused his sad downfall.
Sweet tender sire, alas! Alas! Your fled
Mortality has ranked you with the dead.
Cold, cold's the bed wherein you now do sleep
Damp, damps your couch, which often makes me weep
One kind reflection yields me great content
No one that knew you but does not lament
No more you'll wipe the tear from sorrows eye
Extend your gift or stop the orphans cry
Low here your frame lies buried in the mould
Lord Jesus Christ have mercy on your soul.
                    Amen.

A curious acrostic epitaph.

Also the remains of Hugh son of the above
James McDonnell
Who died 14th January 1846 aged 27 years and
his daughter
Mary died 3rd July aged 23 years and the above
Catherine McDonnell who died 7th July 1849 aged 56 years.

BALLINDOON ABBEY, CO. SLIGO

Terence MacDonagh lies within this grave
That says enough for all that's Generous, Brave
Fasecious, Friendly, Witty, Just and Good
In the Lov'd name is fully understood
For it includes what ever we Virtue call
And is the Hieroglyphic of them all.
Pray for ye soul of Ellen O'Rourke
His wife who caused ye monument to
Be erected in the year 1713

CLIFTON STREET CEMETERY, BELFAST

Sacred to the memory of
Thomas Cordukes
Who died October 24th 1825
aged 28 years
In silent anguish, Oh my spouse,
When I recall thy worth;
Thy [lovely] lifetime's early end,
I fell estranged from earth;
My soul desires with thine to rest,
Supremely and for ev[er b]lest

BALLYCHERIHAN, CO. TIPPERARY

This Tomb
Was erected by the only daughter
Of Mr. JOHN SMITH late of Clonmel
The fond and afflicted widow
Of Mr VALENTINE BROWN
Who died the 28th March 1801 in the 33rd yr
Of his age
He was a man of unassuming manners
RELIGIOUS PROBITY & CHRISTIN PIETY

Stranger, you knew him not, but still draw near
And for an honest MAN let fall a friendly tear.

In Fond and loving
Memory of
My darling husband
MARMADUKE WELPLY
CUNNINGHAM
Who fell asleep
11th July 1907
aged 41 years.
Rest on my darling thy labours o'er,
Thy willing hands will toil no more
Forget you, no! I never will
Though years roll by we love you still.
Erected
By his wife
HANNAH ISABELLA
Who so soon joined him
10th January 1908.
Aged 36 years.

Lovely and pleasant in their lives, and in
Their death they were not divided.
II Sam 1.23

Wives

Essy Pelan
Died on the anniversary of her
Birthday
1st March, 1833 Aged 21 years.
Separated below...united above
For love is strong as death,
Solomon's song 8:6
Thou wert faithful unto death.
Rev: 2.10.
Thy love was wonderful passing the
Love of women
2 Sam: I : 26
I weep the more because I weep in vain
Thou wert my life,
The ocean to the river of my
Thoughts
Which terminated all

BALLINCOLLIG MILITARY GRAVEYARD, CO. CORK

Wife of Captain J. Liddle, aged 38 years
Her toils are passed,
Her work is done,
And She is Truly Blessed.
She fought the fight,
The Victory Won.
She is fully Blessed,
Her entered into Rest.
(erected by her sorrowing husband)

THE CORD CEMETERY, DROGHEDA, CO. LOUTH

Erected by Richard Rielly of Drogheda
In memory of his wife Christina
Who died 15th July 1849 aged 36 years.

Mourn not for me I am dead and gone
My loving husband Gods will be done
And on my Children pity take
And care them for their Mother's sake

Also his brother Charles who died 5th September 1841
aged 34 years

**HERE LYETH THE BODY OF SUSANA
THE WIFE OF CAP ROBERT RUS
SEL WHO DEPARTED THIS LIFE
THE 22 DAY OF DECEMBER AN° DNI
1672,
AETATIS SVAE 64.**

Entered in mould here lyeth she
Who for a time was wife to three.
In constant sorte she livd awhile
With one whose name was Rich. Stile
When Stiles the thread of time had wove,
She weded was to Stephen Cloue,
And with him livd an all content,
Until his Glass was also spent.
This virtuous piece when Clove was ded
Did Captaine Robert Russell wed,
Where she her virtues did display,
Till death did call her debt to pay.
Her life on earth was good was blest
In sweete repose she here doth rest;
Till trumps shall sound hence to away
With Christ to live in blise for aye.

Erected by Owen Smith of Drogheda.

Low here dose lie relas'd from worly care
The dear remains of a sweet lovly fair
Whose sole desire was plas'd in heaven above
Her God alone was all her Joy and Love.
Her happy life was one continued scene
Of Prayer devotion vertue and esteem.
Of her sweet lord and heavens bright
Queenlike wife.
Till her dear soul did soar above the skeys
There evermore to sing eternal praise
To her good God and bless his glorious way.
As she has done when in this life confind
But now her voice is treble more refind
Just in the eleventh year of her age
This child of God dropt off this mortal stage
And bid adue to this frail world of sin
Where no real joy is to be had within.
So much to the memory of Ann Smith
Daughter of the above Owen Smith
She died June 21st 1818
Also his son Peter he died in the 5th
Year of his age

In the churchyard of Drogheda are some curious figures carved in stone against the east wall, with three martlets and the following epitaph:

O! cruel Death,
How could you be so unkind
To take him before,
And leave me behind;
You should have taken both of us, if either,
Which would have been more pleasant to the survivor.
Patrick O'Nell obiit an: aet 30.

CARLINGFORD, CO. LOUTH

Erected
To the memory of ANN
The Beloved wife of
JAMES DUFF, who departed
This life the 23rd of July 1846.
Aged 61 years
Afflictions sore long time I bore
Physicians were in vain
Until it pleased the great I am
To ease me of my pain.

HERE LYETH BVRIED THE BODY
OF MRS MARY STOUGHTON WIFE TO
MR ANTHONY STOUGHTON OF THE CITY OF
DUBLIN, GENT., & DAUGHTER TO THE RIGHT WORP-
FULL HENRY MAINWAIRINGE OF THE CITIE OF
KILKENNY ESQ. & ONE OF THE MASTERS OF HIS
MATTIES HGH COURT OF CHANCERY IN IRELAND WHO
DIED IN CHILDBIRTH OF THE THIRD CHILD NAMED HENRY
THE THIRD DAY OF JANVARY 1631 & ARE BOTH HERE
INTOMBED TOGTHER

Epitaph

A virtuous mother and her new-borne Sonne
Parted ere tomb and end where they begun
Shee from her bearing-bed, hee from the wombe
Exchanged their living graves for this dead tombe
This pile and Epitaph seeme vainly spent
Goodness reares her a surer monument
No curious hand can cut, no lab'ring head
Bring more to praise her than the life shee lead
Bemone that readest! And live well (as shee)
Soe shalt thou want nor tombe nor elegie.

FOXHALL CEMETERY, CARRIGEEN, LENAMORE,
CO. LONGFORD

**Scared to the memory of Dora, wife of Emmet G Fox Esqr
Who died Christmas Day 1867, aged 26 years,
Death Shuck the Dart
And pitying sighed.
And virtue groaned
When Dora died.**

CASTLETOWN GRAVEYARD, DUNDALK, CO. LOUTH

**This monument was erected by Arthur Hampton
In memory of Mrs Anne Hampton who departed
This life the 20 September 1776 aged 56 yrs.
Weep not for me who here do lie
Weep for yourselves who are to die**

In memory of
Louisa, wife of Fredk Falkiner
Who died 27th of April 1817
Aged 56
The rectitude of Her Disposition
Was equalled by
The mildness of her Temper
And the kindness of Her Affections,
And all were so excellent that in 22 Years
Her Partner never saw Her in ill humour
Never heard Her express an unkind word
Or do an act
That Reason might not approve
Blessed with such a Companion
Possessed of so true a Friend
What should Her Husband fear
But Her Loss?
What should He Dread
But to survive Her?

CLONAGOOSE, CO. CARLOW

I.H.S.
Erected by Pat Cloney in memory of his wife
Anne Cloney,
Alias Byrne who depd. this life February 16, 1832,
aged 50 years.

Like you in this world I had my day,
Remember death and for me pray.
May she rest in peace. Amen.

ROSSCARBERY CHURCH, CO. CORK

In memory of
Sarah Smith,
Who died May 14 1822 aged 22 years.

My husband dear my life is past
My love for you did so long last.

KILMANAGHAN GRAVEYARD, CO. OFFALY

This tomb is erected by Edward Bor Esq.
In memory of his wife Jane Bor alias Peacock,
who departed this life Feb. 10th 1765, aged 22 years.
To me was given to dye,
To thee tis given to Live;
Alas one moment acts us even,
Mark how impartial is
The will of Heaven

PASSLANDS GRAVEYARD, MONASTEREVIN, CO. KILDARE

This Unique and lasting Monument
Erected by Peter Gerrard
In Memory of his beloved Wife
Bridget
Who departed this life December the 4th 1835
Aged 50 years.
She's Dead but only Dead to this
Sad deceitful World of ours.
She's Gone to Share that Heavenly Bliss
For which She Laboured her Mortal Hours
Ah Well she felt those passing Scenes
Those Empty Baubles that Mortals Cherish
Were but as Fleeting farey's dreams
Which live the Night and at Morn Perish.

Here lie the remains of
ARABELLA M. FRENCH
Wife of Edward FRENCH. Bella
Co Roscommon
Who departed this life February
17th 1874 aged 70 years.
she expressed a desire to be placed in
the same tomb with her aunt M.A.
IRWIN but the erection of the new
Church rendered the tomb inaccessible.
R.I.P.

RATHVILLY, CO. CARLOW

To the memory of MRS ANNE WHITTY
Here lie beneath this marble stone consign'd
Wife, Mother, Sister, Christian all combined
Each station gently fill'd by God approv'd
She died lamented, as she lived beloved
The shaft by which the fatal blow was given
No sting inflicting sent her soul to Heaven.
Died 22 Feb 1826

ATHLONE ABBEY, CO. WESTMEATH

God takes the good
Too good on earth to stay
And leaves the bad
Too bad to take away.
O Lord have Mercy on the
Soul of Mary Keighry alias
Curley Departed this life
September the 1st 1832 aged
36 years Erected to her
Memory by her husband
Edward Keighry also to the
Memory of four of his
Children that died young
May they rest in peace Amen.

ATHLONE ABBEY, CO. WESTMEATH

Ann Mooney alias Mulcham
Died 9 February 1825 aged 32

Here let her scared dust remain
Who brake the indissoluble chain
Of all my dearest fondest hopes resigned
Virtues nature to Him aspire
Who none has sought in vain desire
But crowned their hopes with heavenly joys assigned.
Erected by her husband.

Lord have mercy on the soul of Alexander
McDonnell who Departed this life March
The 7th 1828 aged 36 years. Also
O Lord have Mercy on the Soul of
Mary McDonnell Allias Muldoone
Who departed this life April
26th 1826 Aged 32 years
also her children Thomas
who died May 14th 1814
aged 1 Year. James who
died May 21st 1823 Aged 5 years.

Though now she lies a victim to the grave
The best and kindest wife God ever gave
Her memory lives embalmed in filial tears
Till those she parted joins her in the spheres
Where bliss celestial reigns nor joy nor woe
Nor all those griefs which clouds this world below.

This monument was Ercd by her affectionate
Husband Alexr McDonnell as a tribute of
Respect for the love he entertained for a
Most Amiable wife and affectionate mother
May she rest in peace.

Men of God

KILGEEVER CHURCH, CO. MAYO

The Rev. Wm. Joyce P.P. Louisburgh
Having paid out of his own private funds
A debt of £200 incurred in the erection of the Presbytery
Which he now leaves free forever to his successors
But on condition that 6 Masses will be said annually for
ever for his intentions
We approve of the above
John Archbishop of Tuam 16th June 1888

CASHEL CATHEDRAL, CO. TIPPERARY

Miler Magrath

Patrick, the glory of our isle and gown,
First a bishop in the see of down
I wish that I, succeeded him in place
As bishop, had an equal grace,
I served thee, England, fifty years in jars
And pleased thy princes in the midst of wars.
Here where I'm placed I'm not; and thus the case is
I'm not in both, yet am in both the places.

INNISCARRA GRAVEYARD, CO. CORK

**Here lyeth the Revd Thomas Patrickson, M.A., who
Reseigned the cure of Inniscarra for a better Country,
July 16, 1748, aged 45 years.**

**His Sacred Ashes here Abide,
Who in God's Service Lived and Died;
But now by Christ advanced Higher
He Serves in the Celestial Choir.**

SEAGOE CHURCH, PORTADOWN, CO. ARMAGH

**Sacred to the memory of the Rev. Richard Buckby, who
Departed this life January 18th 1796, aged 72 years, late
Vicar of the parish of Segoe 33 years, a sincere friend
To the family drops a tear of sorrow for the departure
Of the above worthy and honourable character.**

To the memory
Of Revd Peter Richard Clinch
Roman Catholic pastor of this Parish
Who died on the 29th December 1792
In the 29th year of his age
And the 5th of his mission
In humble hope with Christ again to rise
Beneath this stone the friend, the pastor lies.
His manners open, elegant and sage;
His youth rever'd like venerable age;
His charity, which oft her all bestow'd,
And of in sorrows for the helpless flow'd,
Alas! Could not reverse the mournful doom;
And torture sunk him to an early tomb.
Here laid in peace, his honour'd ashes rest;
Here all with tenderness his virtues own
And grateful near this monumental stone.

OUR LADY'S ISLAND, CO. WEXFORD

Here lieth the body of
The Revd Andrew Mc
Cormack depd 31st
May 1781 aged 58 years
May the lord have mercy on his soul Amen

The World is a jest, as all things
Shew it; I thought so once, But
Now I know it.

The Murphys

In a corner of the churchyard surrounded by a wall the following inscriptions are carved on three different headstones. At the entrance to these graves, visitors are greeted by the inscription:

The burial apartment of the ancient family of the
Murphys
Of Lacken

INSIDE:

Here amidst his friends doth lye
The remains of Mr E. Murphy
Who in 1741, on the first day
Did the great debt of nature pay,
Precisely at the age of fifty-seven,
He quit this life, and soar'd for heaven,
Then let it be each readers prayer,
That he has got admission there.
Amen.

Here lies Mary, Edmond's wife,
Who spent a happy proper life
She was a comely well-bred woman,
Descended from Fermoy and Shannon.
Her parents were a Roche and Boyle,
Which cannot this assertion foyle,
When of this stage in 1747
My God receive her soul in heaven.
Amen.

Here's Rev. Bryan, the son of both,
To his church did pledge his troth.
See by the Cross, Host and Chalice,
The emblems of his sacred office.
Years thirty one, he filled this district,
Which numbers doubled closed his exit.
In 1779, the last day of May,
Subtil death snatched him away.
Let's wish him requiescat in peace.
Amen.

Sailors

Born to a course of Manly action free,
I dauntless trod ye fluctuating sea
In Pompous War or happier Peace to bring
Joy to my Sire and honour to my King.
And much by favour of the God was done
Ere half the term of human life was run.
One fatal night, returning from the bay
Where British fleets ye Gallic land survey,
Whilst with warm hope my trembling heart beat high,
My friends, my kindred, and my country nigh,
Lasht by the winds the waves arose and bore
Our Ship in shattered fragments to the shore.
There ye flak'd surge opprest my darkening sight,
And there my eyes for ever lost the light.

Captain George Colvill of the Private Ship
of War 'Amazon,' and only son of
Robert Colvill of Bangor, was wrecked
near this ground 25th February 1780, in
ye 22nd year of his age.

Sacred to the memory of
Ambrose Lennon and Margaret his wife,
The former having foundered in a hurricane
in the West Indies on board his Majesty's ship
Barbadoes with all the crew in the year 1780.
The latter departed this life the 5th March 1804
aged 71 years.
Oh stormy ocean
That deprived him first of life
Long lingered and then died
His virtuous wife.
This stone erected by their son Captain John Lennon.

ST MARY'S, NEW ROSS, CO. WEXFORD

Sacred to the memory of
Evan Williams
The son of Evan Williams of Nevan Caernarvonshire who was
Unfortunately drowned the 17th of August 1845 aged
44 years.

In perfect health I met my death
In bloom of youth it took me hence
In peace I lived In peace I died
I prayed for life but God denied.

Captain William Stewart was the well-liked commander of the brig *Mary Russell* of Cork — until he murdered seven crewmen during a period of paranoid madness on a voyage back from Barbados in June 1828. Some time after setting sail, the captain began to show signs of strangeness. Convinced his fellow Corkmen were planning to mutiny and take hold of the ship, he decided to act first and slaughter them. He carried out his gruesome plan with cunning subtlety. In order to allay his fears, the unsuspecting crew willingly submitted to being bound hand and foot, thinking that by humouring Stewart they could prevail on him to get some sleep. No sooner had they been rendered powerless than the captain produced a crowbar and beat out their brains in a frenzy of madness.

At his trial in Cork, survivors recounted all the horrific details of the voyage. The captain was found guilty but insane and spent the rest of his life in lunatic asylums in Dublin and Cork before dying in 1873.

A tombstone erected in Marmullane Graveyard, Passage West, Co. Cork recalls the tragedy:

This stone was erected
By PATRICK CONNELL in
Memory of his Brother
TIMOTHY CONNELL who was
murdered on board of the
MARY RUSSELL 22nd June 1828
Also as a burial place for himself
And Family
You gentle reader that do pass this way
Attend a while, adhere to what I say.
By murder vile I was bereft of life
And parted from two lovely babes and wife.
By CAPTAIN STEWART I met an early doom
On board the MARY RUSSELL the 22nd June.
Forced from the world to meet my God on High
With whom I hope to reign eternally Amen.
Aged 28 years.

JOHN HALL OF DUN LAOGHAIRE, CO. DUBLIN

Through Boreas' spight and Neptune's foom,
I have ranged ye Ocean wide, by God's decree
It is my doom
Oct 3rd, 1750

CORD CEMETERY, DROGHEDA, CO. LOUTH

The family burial place of Captain James Fay and posterity.
Three sons that was drowned at sea,
But no buoy or beacon marks their graves.
They lie beneath the waves.
And the sweet flowers that deck the spring,
Bloom on my peaceful grave.

FAITHLEGG CEMETERY, CO. WATERFORD

This stone was erected by Mrs Mary Dinn of Passage as a mark of her burial ground and in memory of her father Nicholas, her mother Honora, her brother Martin, her sisters, and particularly of her brother William Dinn alias Doyle, who sailed round the Globe with Captn Cook, and was present at the death of that great Circumnavigator at Owhyee, and who died respected and regretted at Stoke near Devonport in England in June 1840, having spent a long life as a Warrant Officer in the service of his country. May they rest in peace.

John Cullen, mariner, died in 1878 aged 62.

**For 35 years and upwards
I fought king Alcohol.
With heart in hand
And tongue in a foreign land.
And I won the victory.
I am back again in the old country
Fighting the same old king
And so far I am victorious.**

**Charles McAlasters Burr
Ing Place
Here lies the
Boddy of John
His son died 11
March 1803
Aged 18 years
'Your ship
Love is mor
Ed head and
Starn for a fuldiew'**

CASTLETOWN GRAVEYARD, DUNDALK, CO. LOUTH

This monument was erected
by order of Patrick Byrne,
of Castletown, esq.,
in the year of our Lord 1791

Tho' Neptunes waves & Boras' blasts
Have tossed me to and fro
Yet after all I am come at last
To harbour here below
Where I hope my bones will rest
Unto Judgement Day shall be.
O good Christians who read this
I Beg you will pray for me

ST MATTHEW'S CHURCHYARD, RINGSEND, DUBLIN 4

Sacred to the memory of Henry Totty,
late Commander of The Brigg Hawk of Chester,
who was upwards of 40 years trading
from that city and Liverpool to this Port.
For honesty and integrity he might be equalle'd,
but not exceeded.
He departed this life the 3rd day of July, 1799,
aged 60 years.
Reader,
remember an honest man is the noblest work of God

Here lieth the body of Grace Lusk alias DRINNAN, wife of Capt Arthur Lusk, who departed this life 15th August 1733 aged 33 Also Ann Lusk alias CUPPLES who departed this life 3 July 1802 aged 77 Also Captain Arthur Lusk who circumnavigated the globe with Lord Anson, he departed this life the 9th of April 1808 aged 94 years Farewell, son of Neptune, farewell, Life's tempests thou long hast endured, Misfortune's rude waves now may swell, For thou art in harbour, safe moor'd, Light lie the green turf on thy breast, May thy sleep be unbroken and soft, Till the Archangel calls thee from rest, By piping all sailors aloft, Then joyfully may'st thou set sail, And gain that Elysian shore, Where the storm or the billows shall fail, To disturb thy repose any more Also his daughter Milinda Lusk alias SMITH alias CAIRNS who departed this life 22d July 1817 aged 66 years Also Mary RUSSEL, formerly of Holywood, who departed this life 5 Feb 1830 aged 96 years.

WHITECHURCH, CO. DOWN

**Dedicated by Jane McCall to the memory of her beloved
husband Isaac McCall, mariner, late of Ballywalter, who was
accidentally drowned at Londonderry
4th March 1832 aged 34 years
O hapless youth, how sudden was thy doom,
That dawning morn how lightly did'st thou tread,
And little thought that in a watery tomb,
At days decline thou shouldst repose thy head,
But now thy happy spirit dwells on high,
And guardian angels pointed out thy way,
Thou'lt rise at last when time itself shall die,
And live with God through never-ending day.**

FAHAN CHURCH, CO. DONEGAL

**In memory of
HORATIO NELSON
late midshipman of H.M.S. Endymion
an amiable youth who breathed his last at
Fahan House in the 18th year of his age.
Could friendship have prolonged his days
he had lived.
Born at Burnham Thorpe in the County of Norfolk.
Died November 17th 1811.
NOMENQUE ERIT INDELEBILE NOSTRIS**

Here lieth the Remains of
Captn Robert Bryan, late of the
Margaret of Liverpool who
Unfortunately lost his Life in a
Violent gale of wind on this Coast
The 24th of March 1810 Aged 32 years
At Anchor here my Body lies
Till the last trump shall bid it rise
My flesh shall hear the living word
Then quit my Tomb to meet the Lord
Dear Wife forbear to mourn your loss
The Tempests now ceas'd to toss
I've launch'd into the eternal Main
Where we must shortly meet again
This stone is placed here by desire of his
Disconsolate Widow as a tribute of respect.

DONAGHADEE GRAVEYARD, CO. DOWN

[With an anchor carved at the top]

Beneath this stone lies Daniel Saul
Who round the world's terraqueous ball
Has sailed to every land was known
Now under hatches lies at home.
Anchor'd among his kindred mould
Dreads neither storms nor seas that roll
Brought to by death's correcting rod
Sets sail again to meet his God.
He died 24th August 1820 aged 42 years.

LARNE GRAVEYARD, CO. ANTRIM

Here [lieth] the body of William M[unr]o who departed
This life [………..] aged 66 years al[so………
………] Jane Peyto who dep[arted] this life Dec 8th
1[7]97 [aged] 43 years, and his Daughter Ann Ferres
who died Jan 20 1802 aged 44 [yea]rs Also his son
David [who] departed this life [……………]
1804 aged 48 years […………] wife Mary Munro who
[depa]rted this life 19th July 1804 aged 90 years.

No more Munros shall cross the Tropick Line
Nor bid his crew defy the Polar Wave
Or spread more sail to leave their foe behind
Here lies the landlock'd in the silent grave.

MONKNEWTON, DROGHEDA, CO. LOUTH

Erected by Patrick Kelly
Of the Town of Drogheda, Mariner.
In Memory of his Posterity.

Also the above Patrick Kelly
who departed this Life the 12th August 1844.
Aged 60 years.
Requiescat in Pace

Soldiers

Mr William Charter Esqre.
Of the County of Northumberland
Late a Captain in the 16th Regiment of Foot
Who departed this life
October the 21th 1762
Aged 61 years
There needs no Statue to adorn this Dust,
Here Charter lies and Honour in his Bust.

In memory of
Lieut Colonel Brown
Of Breaffy in this county
4th Kings Own Regiment
then of 92nd Highlanders and 98th Foot
her served King and Country
in the expedition to Sweden
the retreat of Corumna, the lines of Torres Vedras
Redhina, Fuentes D'Onor
Ciudad-Rodriga and the siege of Badajos
Where he was severely wounded
The battles of Quatrebas and Waterloo
There received three wounds from which he lay
48 hours for dead on the field of victory
He died at Breaffy
20th Novr. 1849

HEADFORD CHURCHYARD, CO. GALWAY

Here lies the Body of
Joseph Levered, Privte Soldr
2nd Bn 12th Regt who was born
at Wallingford, Berkshire, in
1796, and was killed by a stab
in the back in a Public House
in Headford on 23rd Dec 1817 aged 21.
This stone was Erected by
His sorrowing Comrades as a
Proof of their Esteem.
Reader, beware of drunken
Midnight Meetings lest the
same fate await you.

KILBROGAN CHURCH, BANDON, CO. CORK

From the rude world's campaigns, the much-admired,
Legard! The daring soldier whose fond name,
Shall ever flourish in the book of fame.
Whose fair example might alone depaint,
What 'tis to be a military saint.
True to god, his prince, his friend, his word,
Rare ornaments, but fit t' adorn the sword.

Beneath lieth the body of Edward Legard, lieutenant,
To Captain Robert Hyliard, who died 6th of January, 1678.

MALLOW CHURCHYARD, CO. CORK

I.H.S.
His delight was the bottle.
Here lies interred Brave Sergt. O'BRYAN,
For implements of war he was inclined,
The Vth Dragoons was his delight.
He followed them both day and night,
And in regard to his Loyalty,
This stone was erected by the Vth Royal Irish Dgs.
He departed this life May 11th, 1797,
Aged 60.

BALLINCOLLIG MILITARY GRAVEYARD, CO. CORK

Bomb. Charles Mason. Aged 22 years
Comrades see a Soldiers Grave
Tread Lightly O'er this sod.
And Now that you
Your soul save,
My soul seek
Your earthly Peace with God.

BALLINCOLLIG MILITARY GRAVEYARD, CO. CORK

Sgt. Joseph Bednall, aged 28
Much regretted by the Officers,
Non-Comm. Officers, and the Corps
His race is run, His Battles o'er,
Ended in his last campaign.
He ne'er shall see another shore,
Nor ever march again.

ST FIAAC'S, CLONEGAL, CO. CARLOW

There is a headstone with a quaint representation of a
soldier in ancient uniform — knee-breeches and
stockings, and a gun on his shoulder, with the
inscription:

Here Lieth the body of the
Spaerited volunteer Henry
Browne, Departed 14th May,
1784, aged 26 years.

Underneath lies the body of Frederick, Duke of Schomberg, slain at the Battle of the Boyne, in the year 1690. The Dean and the Chapter of this Church again and again besought the Heirs of the Duke to cause some monument to be here erected to his memory. But when, after many entreaties by letters and by friends they found they could not obtain this request, they themselves placed this stone; only that the indignant Reader may know where the ashes of Schomberg are deposited. Thus did the Fame only of his Virtue obtain more for him from strangers, than nearness of blood from his own family.

The Dean of St Patrick's, Jonathan Swift, penned this epitaph in the 1720s when the Duke of Schomberg's family refused to put up a memorial for him.

MOUNT JEROME, DUBLIN

**An Col Tomas Mac Conmara
Croisin, Co an Clair
30-9-1916 go 23-9-1977
A Gentleman by the Grace of God
And an Act of Parliament.**

CHRISTCHURCH, CASTLEBAR, CO. MAYO

**In loving memory of
Major Harry Francis Chads M.C.
the Border Regiment
who was accidentally killed at Castlebar
on 28th August 1920
whilst flying on duty
Erected by the officers, non commissioned officers
and men of the 2nd Battalion**

ST PAUL'S, NORTH KING STREET, DUBLIN 7

**LIEUT WILLM GORDON, AGED 11 YEARS,
DEPARTED THIS LIFE SUDDENLY, BEING
ONLY FOUR HOURS ILL, AUGUST 3RD, 1796
THE ONLY SON OF LIEUT WM GORDON,
AS ALSO HIS MOTHER WHO FROM GRIEF
FOLLOWED HIM ON THE 8TH DAY OF FEBRY,
1797, AGED 16 YEARS.**

Take a glance at this inscription and wonder at how
mathematically incorrect it is.

In or near the garrison-town of Athlone, an epitaph was placed over the remains of a sergeant-major who had the reputation of being a severe disciplinarian. Evidently the composer had reason to regret his severity, and to feel anything but sorry for the demise of the martinet, as the lines show:

> Here lies our bold sergeant-major,
> To flog a man he was always aiger;
> Here he lies, without sheet or blanket,
> Stiff as a crutch, the Lord be thanked!

> Sacred to the Memory of
> John Ingham late Quartr Maftr
> 7th Dn Guards who departed
> this life 22nd July 1817 Aged
> 62 Years
> Also of Elizabeth Ingham his Wife
> who died 2nd Jany 1818 Aged 58 years
> This Stone was erected as
> A tribute of filial Love
> by their Daughter
> Anne Ingham.

On the back of the stone is the following:

The Governors of the Louth Hospital
have caused the following extract,
from their Journals to be engraved
on the Tomb Stone of their late Warden
and Matron
JOHN and ELIZA INGHAM
That we have juft cause to lament
their deceace
That their conduct as Servants of the
Public was uniformly regulated by the
Stricteft senfe of integrity and oeconomy and as
Warden of the Sick and Maimed by the
tender feelings of tendernies
That in the care of the House generally they
eftablished an admirable System of order
alfo of cleanlinefs and were Both in their own
behaviour Sober, Respectable and Decorous.
That we are very desirous to uphold their
example in all these respects for the
imitation of those who may at any time
hereafter succeed them.

CHURCH OF THE IMMACULATE CONCEPTION, CAMOLIN,
CO. WEXFORD

As the days roll by, this day we do recall.
The noonday sun. The twittering of strange birds.
The brown meandering stream, that heard the din of battle
And carried your cries to history, to join the brave.
That swords be turned into ploughshares.

Erected by the people of Camolin and comrades
To the memory of Trooper Edward Gaffney, Norrismount.
Killed in the Congo (Zaire) on the 13th September, 1961.
In the cause of world peace.

OLD FERMOY GRAVEYARD, CO. CORK

Erected by the Non-Commissioned Officer, Drummers
& Private Men
Of Captain Sankey's Company 1st Batt'n
Of His Majesty's IX Regiment of Infantry.
To the memory of James Bromlow who depart'd
This life the IX day of Aug'st AE 24 yrs.
Comrades reflect on your eternal state,
Repent your sins before it's too late.
Life is uncertain, as you Daily see.
Death may soon summon you to follow me.

Erected by the Sergeants of His Majesty's 9th Reg't of Foot
Sacred to the memory of William Smallbrook late Sergeant
in the said Corps
Who departed this life on the 13th April 1807 aged 35 yrs.
Regretted and Revered by all. A good soldier
And honest Comrade & a tender Friend.
Stay generous Comrade and shed a tear
For one that oft shed for his comrades dear
His march being now performed and at the Halt
And may his soul be found without a Fault
In hopes to be selected amongst the number
When the last Trumpet will awake from Slumber
And trust to meet that Lenity in Heaven
Which to his Comrades he has often given.

Returned to his native land
lieth all that was mortal of
Lieutenant Taffe McGovern,
Late of Northumberland Regiment of the Fencible Infantry.
He fell in a duel on the 2nd March 1802,
in the 23 year of his age.
If the esteem and regard of his brother officers
who have erected this stone to the memory
could assist his soul in its flight to heaven,
its ascent must have been rapid and its reception good

Two German soldiers lie here and the inscriptions on their memorials are in German and English.

**In memory of
Cristophe Koch Rifleman
in the 5th Company of the 1st Light Infantry Battalion
Kings German Legion. He was born in Goettingen
in the Electorate of Hanover, Germany
and died the 16th July at Tullamore aged 23 years.
He lived like a Christian and
a true Soldier and died performing his duty.**

**Sacred to the memory of
Fredk. Willm. Baron Olderhausen
late a Captain in His Majesty's 1st German Dragoons.
Born the 15th March 1776 at Verden in
The Electorate of Hanover and
departed this life at Tullamoore
the 22nd of December 1808.**

**The bonds of husband, father, friend
are early loosed in a foreign country.
Thou sleepest the solemn sleep of death.
This monument speaks no lie,
the graving-tool of truth carves these lines
Thou wert true, noble, loyal, brave.**

KILLANIN OLD, CO. GALWAY

**Sacred to the memory of Major
Thomas William Poppleton of the
53rd Reg an officer immensely
distinguished and brave accomplished
and Christian soldier. He served in
India, in Egypt, on the Peninsula
And was honoured by the esteem of Napoleon
who was under his personal charge for two years
in St. Helena
obiit October the 9th 1827
aged 52 years.**

ST NAHI'S, TANEY, CO. DUBLIN

**Sacred to the memory of Lieut-Col Wm. Cowell,
C.B., late of the 42nd Royal highlanders, whose
Premature death was occasioned by severe campaigns
And wounds received in the Peninsula
During the war; he died 24th September, 1827, aged
45 years.**

ST PAUL'S, NORTH KING STREET, DUBLIN 7

LIEUT. COL. AUGUSTUS CUYLER,
Chief Commissioner of the Metropolitan Police of the
City of Dublin, decd.,
14th June, 1837, aged 40 years,
formerly in the Coldstream Regiment of Foot

Farewell to him whom youthful valour drew
To seek a soldier's fame at Waterloo.

MOUNT JEROME, DUBLIN

To the beloved memory of
Colonel Hans Garrett Moore VC C.B.
Late Commanding Officer Argyle and Sutherland
Highlanders
And formerly Connaught Rangers
Who was accidentally drowned in Loch Derg
During a gale October 7th 1889
Age 54 years
He served with distinction in the Indian Mutiny, the
Ashantee War 1874
The Kaffir War 1877–1878
And the Egyptian War 1882.
He received the Victoria Cross
For endeavouring to save the life of a
Soldier left alone surrounded by Kaffirs.
This monument is erected by his sorrowing sister
HM Bird.

ST ANNE'S, BALLYSHANNON, CO. DONEGAL

William Urquhart.
Late captain in the Royal Essex Regiment of Infantry.
Son of late William Urquhart of Meldrum, Esq.,
Aberdeenshire, Scotland,
died September 29th 1798, aged 42 years.
This memorial was erected by his disconsolate widow.
How loved, how honoured once, avail thee not
To whom related or by whom begot;
A heap of dust alone remains of thee,
Tis all thou art and all the great shall be.

ST JAMES' GRAVEYARD, JAMES' STREET, DUBLIN 8

12760 Private
T. Murphy
Of the Royal Dublin Fusiliers
31st May 1915 age 35
Gone But Never Forgotten.

Exiles

James Bronterre O'Brien
Departed this life
December 23rd
1864
Aged 67
His life was grand
His death was sad and drear

Sacred to the Memory
Of
JAMES BARRY,
Who
To strong natural powers of mind
Added the intellectual rules
(The only rules he ever consulted or possessed),
which spring from
Learning, Philosophy, and Religion;
Hence,
Both as a painter and a writer, a lofty conception,
A moral tendency and a Grecian taste,
Enobled, sanctified, and adorned
All his works.
Born at Cork, 1741,
Died in London, 1806.

RANGOON CANTONMENT CEMETERY, BURMA

DAN MATTHEW McCARTHY IGO
Born Roscommon 24th January 1848.
Died 19th June 1923.
Peacefully sleeping, resting at last,
Life weary trials and suffering past.
In silence he suffered, in patience bore,
Till God called him home, to suffer no more.

PUTNEY VALE CEMETERY, LONDON

In Proud
And Ever Loving Memory Of
PETER CHEYNEY
Actor · Soldier · Author
Died 26th June 1951

ST MICHAEL'S CHURCHYARD, STINSFORD, DORSET

**CECIL
DAY LEWIS
1904–1972
Poet Laureate
Shall I be Gone Long?
For Ever And A Day
To Whom There Belong?
Ask The Stone To Say
Ask My Song**

JOHN LEWIS, SHENANDOAH VALLEY, AUGUSTA COUNTY, VIRGINIA

**Here lie the remains of JOHN LEWIS,
who slew the Irish Lord, settled Augusta County,
located the Town of Staunton, and furnished five sons
to fight
the battles of the American Revolution.
He was the son of Andrew Lewis and Mary Calhoun
and was born in Donegal County, Ireland in 1678,
and died Feb'y Ist, 1762, aged 84 years.
He was a true patriot and a friend of liberty throughout
the world.
Mortalitate Relicta Vivit Immortalitate Inductus.**

MARY 'MOTHER' JONES
Born May 1, 1830
Died November 30, 1930
She gave her life to the world of labor, her blessed soul to heaven.
God's finger touched her and now she sleeps.

From Kohat in north-west Pakistan, near the border with Afghanistan, comes an interesting tombstone epitaph of an Irish surgeon:

Here rest the remains of MICHAEL HEALY, Apothecary in the Hon'ble Company's service, destroyed by the Afreedees, 23rd March, 1850.
Michael Healy was an Irishman, highly gifted with talents, energy and ambition. Foiled in his aim and weary of struggle with the world, he ardently sought that repose which he has here found.

The Afreedees were an Afghan tribe, and the 'Hon'ble Company' mentioned was the Honourable East India Company. Dublin-born Healy was travelling to join the 1st Punjab Infantry at Kohat when he was attacked six miles from his destination. He died next day. His daughter Frances who died in 1845, aged only three months, is buried at Agra Cantonment Cemetery.

Kohat Cemetery also has a memorial to another Irishman:

IHS
In memory of ARTHUR U.F. RUXTON Capt. H.M. Bengal Staff
Corps Comdt. 3rd Punjab Infantry born 17th May 1832
who fell nobly at the head of his Regiment
whilst leading an attack against
a stronghold of the Bazoties on 11th March 1868.
For this God is our God for ever and ever
he will be our guide unto death. PSALM XLVIII 14.

AGRA CANTONMENT CEMETERY, INDIA

Sacred to the memory of
JOHN CONWAY Sergeant H.M. 39th Regt.
A native of the city of Limerick, Ireland,
who departed this life on the
7th day of July in the year of our Lord 1843.
Aged 37 years and 5 months.
This tomb was erected by a few of his comrade
sergeants as a mark of their esteem & regard.
Though parted from the friends I loved in this uncertain clime.
I hope we'll meet in Heaven above. It's where there is no crime.
May his soul rest in peace. Amen.

Sacred to the memory of
SERGEANT MAJOR THOMAS REID
3rd Battalion of Artillery.
A native of Tralee, County Kerry, Ireland.
Who departed this life on 16th August 1845.
Aged 41 years.
Leaving a disconsolate widow to mourn his loss.
This tomb was erected by his beloved wife Honora Reid.
RIP.
Before the morning light I'll come
With Magdalen to find
In sighs and tears my Jesus' tomb
And there refresh my mind
My tears upon his grave shall flow
My sighs the garden fill
Then at his feet myself I'll throw
And there I'll seek his will.

To the memory of ISABELLA MAGOWAN
of the town of Newry, Coy. of Down, Ireland and wife of
Private Thomas Magowan of Hs. Ms. 13th Lt. Infantry, who
departed this life on the 1st of April 1829 on her return from
Gorukhpore to Dinapore where she had to attend Mrs
Armstrong wife of Collector Armstrong of that station. She
followed the profession of midwifery
and was greatly regretted and esteemed by the several
respectable Ladies whose patronage she had the honour to
receive. Aged 39 years.
Naked as from the earth we came
And entered life at first
Naked we to the earth return
And mix with kindred dust
'Tis God that lifts our comforts high
or sinks them in the grave.
He giving and when he takes away
He takes but what he gave.
This tablet was erected to her memory by her disconsolate
Husband and five children whom she left to deplore her
loss.

To the memory of
Sir Hans Sloane, Bart.
President of the Royal Society, and the
College of Physicians,
Who in the year of our Lord 1753
Without the least pain of body, and with a
Conscious serenity of mind,
Ended a virtuous and beneficent life,
This monument was erected by his two daughters,
Elizabeth Cadogan and Sarah Stanley.

This memorial was once in St Martin-in-the-Fields in London:

Sacred
To the memory of John Irving Esq.
Of Sligo, Ireland
Surgeon to His Majesty's Forces,
Who died on 22nd of April 1810,
Aged 33 years;
A victim like thousands of our
Gallant Countrymen
To the fatal consequences of the
Unfortunate Expedition to the Scheldt,
Commanded by John, Earl of Chatham

Sacred to the memory
JAMES NIXON
Conductor of the Ordce.
From the County Tyrone, Ireland;
who died Octr. The 9th 1826
aged 45 years.
'Where now alas! my dearest James
Shall Hannah seek for rest
Where but in your saviour's arms
Reclining on his breast.
Oh, may I seek and tread the road,
You sought and ever trod,
And in the end, find that repose,
Which now you have with God.'
This tomb is erected by his disconsolate widow as
a small tribute of her affection.

WESTMINSTER ABBEY, LONDON

SIR
CHARLES
VILLIERS
STANFORD
Born 30th Sept 1852
Died 29th March 1924
A Great
Musician

William Havard,
Died 20 February 1778.

Views of ambition ne'er his hopes employ'd,
Yet honest fame he courted and enjoy'd;
Fair peace he cherish'd, as he hated strife,
And lov'd and liv'd an inoffensive life.
Not unaccomplish'd in the scenic art,
He grac'd the stage, and often reach'd the heart;
From his own scenes he taught distress to flow,
And manly virtue wept for civil woe.
Malevolence and envy he ne'er knew;
He never felt their darts and never threw.
With his best care he form'd into his plan
The moral duties of the social man.

He honour'd virtue, and he lov'd his friend;
Oft from his little to the poor would lend;
And praised his great Creator at his end.

NICHOLSON CEMETERY, DELHI, INDIA

The grave
Of
Brigadier General
John Nicholson
Who led
The assault of Delhi
But fell
In the hour of victory
Mortally wounded
And died
23rd September 1857
Aged 35.

GRACE CHURCH, MASSAPEQUA, LONG ISLAND

Here Lyes interd the Body of Major Thomas Jones,
Who came from Straubane, in the Kingdom of Ireland,
Settled Here, and Died December, 1713.
From Distant Lands To This Wild Waste He Came,
This Seat He Choose, and Here He Fixed His Name,
Long May His Sons This Peace Full Spot Injoy,
And No Ill Fate His Offspring Here Annoy.

Scratched on the back of the tombstone by a wit:

Beneath these stones,
Repose the bones
Of Pirate Jones.
This briny well
Contains the shell
The rest's in Hell.

In Memory of
Thomas Dermody
Who Died 15 July 1802
Aged 28 Years
No Titled Birth Hadst Thou To Boast
Son Of The Desert, Fortune's Child,
Yet Not By Frowning Fortune Cross'd
The Muses On Thy Cradle Smil'd.
Now a Cold Tenant Dost Thou Lie
Of This Dark Cell, All Hushed His Song,
While Friendship Bends With Steaming Eye,
As By Thy Grave She Wends Along,
On Thy Cold Clay Lets Fall A HOLY tear,
And Cries, Though Mute, There Is A Poet Here!
Renovated, 1848
By Some Admirers Of His Genius
Restored, Nov 1886
By Subscription.

In the Masonic Cemetery, San Francisco, is a fine granite pyramid, eight feet square at the base, on the front of which is the following epitaph :

Hugh Whittell. San Francisco.
In the five divisions of the world I have been,
The Cities of Peking and Constantinople I have seen,
On the first Railway I rode, before others were made,
Saw the first telegraph operate, so useful to trade;
On the first steamship, the Atlantic, I crossed,
Suffered six shipwrecks in which lives were lost;
On the first steamer to California I did sail,
And went to China by the first Pacific mail,
After many endeavours my affairs to fix,
A short time I will occupy less than two by six,
A native of Tyrone, Ireland; born 1813.
Died 1874.

On the other side:

All you that chance this grave to see
If you can read English can learn from me.
traveled, read, & studied mankind to know
And what most interested them here below.
The present or the future state & love of power
Envy, fear, love or hate, occupied each wakeful hour.
All would teach, but few would understand,
The greater part know little of God or man.
'Love one another', a very good maxim all agreed,
Learn, labour, wait, if you would succeed.

Erected
By
Philip Ryan, in memory of his brother
MICHEAL RYAN, of Swan Reach
A native of Thornback, Parish of
St Canice's, County Kilkenny, Ireland,
Who has been circumvented of his
Just & legal property, prosecuted
By wilful and corrupt perjury,
Returned guilty by an infamous
And bigoted jury, for being a sincere
Patriot and sentenced wrongfully
By the laws of the land.

Fare you well dear Brother for a while
Hoping the Almighty God has received
Your soul, and on you smile, until his
Herald summonses me to be for ever
Blessed with thee, Amen.

Died on the 28th of Sepr. 1859,
Aged 36 years.

The story behind this gravestone is a fascinating one. Michael Ryan was convicted of murder on flimsy circumstantial evidence on 2 July 1834 and given a life sentence with transportation to Australia. Arriving in that country, he became a member of a chain gang working along the Hunter River. His brother Philip was wealthy and believed in Michael's innocence and decided to come to his aid. He emigrated to Australia as a free settler and bought extensive lands near Morpeth, New South Wales. As a landowner Philip was entitled to have convicts assigned to him as servants so he applied for his brother and got him. Michael subsequently obtained a ticket-of-leave allowing him to settle and his brother helped him buy a farm near Swan Reach. Michael was accidentally drowned in the Hunter River on 28 September 1859 and was buried in East Maitland Cemetery. Philip had the headstone erected and intended to put a lot more on it, but was prevented from doing so by friends who were afraid he too would fall foul of the law.

The following is quoted in many forms and always inaccurately as the epitaph of Lady O'Looney of Pewsey, Bedfordshire.

It is from St George's Chapel, Hanover Square, London. The epitaph is extremely long and I quote it here in abbreviated form:

Sacred to the memory of Mrs. Jane Molony,
Who lies interred in a vault underneath this chapel,
Daughter of Anthony Shee of Castle Bar in the County of Mayo, Esq.,
Who was married to Miss Burke, of Curry, in the said county,
And cousin to the Rt. Hon. Edmund Burke, commonly called the sublime,

Whose bust is here surmounted or subjoined.
The said Jane was cousin to the late Countess of
Buckinghamshire,
And was married to three successive husbands. Thirdly,
Edmond Molony.
The said Mrs. Molony, otherwise Shee, died in London in
January, 1839, aged 74.
She was hot, passionate, and tender, and a highly
accomplished lady and a
Superb drawer in water-colours, which was much admired
in the exhibition room
In Somerset House some years past.
Though lost forever still a friend is dear,
The heart yet pays a tributary tear.
This monument was erected by the deeply afflicted
husband,
The said Edmond Molony, in memory of her great virtue and
talents.
Beloved and deeply regretted by all who knew her.
For such is the kingdom of heaven.

One of the most bizarre church memorials is that of the great Donegal-born eighteenth-century actor Charles Macklin (c.1690–1797) in St Paul's Church in Covent Garden, London. He designed his own memorial to remind others that he had once killed a man. Macklin was notoriously hot-tempered and was always getting into arguments and fights — usually with his fellow actors. In 1735 Macklin accidentally killed another actor during an argument over a wig. In a fit of rage, Macklin lunged at the man with his cane. It went through the man's eye and he died. A remorseful Macklin pleaded self-defence at the trial that followed and escaped hanging, but he never forgot the terrible fight. When he died in 1797, Macklin left instructions that a memorial showing a skull pierced by a knife should be placed above his grave. It can still be seen on the wall of St Paul's. It reads:

Sacred to the Memory
Of CHARLES MACKLIN, Comedian.
This Tablet is Erected
(with the Aid of Public Patronage)
by his affectionate Widow Elizabeth Macklin
Obiit 11th July 1797. Aetatis 107
MACKLIN! The father of the modern stage
Renowned alike for talents and for age
Whose years a Century and longer ran
Who liv'd and dy'd as may become a man
This lasting Tribute to thy Worth receive
Tis all a grateful Public now can give
Their loudest plaudits now no more can move
Yet hear! Thy widow's still small voice of love.

Servants

**To the Memory of WILLIAM RALPH of Kilcarry,
Who died on the 21st Feb 1818 Aged 71 years**

**Guard of the wood in settled low content,
Lived William Ralph, a ramble paid his rent:
A boy, in sportive toil he climbed the trees;
A man, he loved them rustling in the breeze.**

**As he grew old, his old companions spread
A broader, browner shadow o'er his head;
While those he planted shot on high and made
For many a rook an hospitable shade.**

**With this one change, life gently crept away,
A placid stream it flowed from day to day.
His friends & children loved him as the tear
Well spoke, profusely shed upon the bier.**

**If he had faults, thou also hast thy share;
Strike thy one breast, and feel what lurketh there.
He who sees all, shall judge both him and thee;
Repent, for as it falls, so lies the tree.**

William Ralph was wood-ranger to a local landowner
called Henry Tighe, who is said to have written these
lines in memory of him.

Sacred to the memory of
Evan Bevan,
Who died 8th April, 1844,
Aged 32 years.
He lived for nine years coachman
With Major Macan, of Greenmount,
By whom this stone was erected
In memory of a faithful,
honest and excellent servant.

Here lieth the Body of John Young who died on the
14th of March 1841. Aged 83 Years, in the Service of Hugh
Moore Esquire of Eglantine House in whose Family he had
lived for 68 years uniformly evincing the strictest Sobriety,
Fidelity, and attachment. He died trusting in the merits of
his merciful Redeemer. Mr Moore lamenting the loss of a
Servant so faithful and so Trustworthy erects this tribute
to his memory;
a well merited Record of an Example so deserving
of imitation.

Here lieth the body of Alexander McGee, servant to Doctr
Swifte of St Patrick's. His grateful master caused this
monument to be erected in Memory of Discretion, Fidelity
and Diligence in that humble Station. Ob. Mar 24 1723/24.
Aetat. 29.

CARNAGH GRAVEYARD, CO. WEXFORD

Here lies ye body of Mrs Mary
Carrol of ye City of Dublin
Who parted this life at Bantry
Lodge ye 23 Novr 1779.
She was a faithful servant
For many years & on acct of her
Experience, fidelity in the character
of house-keeper this little memorial
has been erected to her memory
& it is hoped the Lord is as
merciful to her.

GLASNEVIN CEMETERY, DUBLIN

To the memory of Anne Devlin (Campbell)
The faithful servant of Robert Emmet who possessed some
rare and many noble qualities, who lived in obscurity and
poverty and died so on the eighteenth day of September
1851 aged 70 years.

DAVIDSTOWN GRAVEYARD, CO. WEXFORD

In memory of
Richard Furlong
Who died 10th September 1859
Aged 23 years
This stone was erected by
Harry Alcock of Wilton Esq
Captain Wexford Regiment
In whose service he was killed by a
Horse falling on him
As a testimonial of respect and esteem.

Actors, Musicians, Writers and Artists

ST NICHOLAS COLLEGIATE CHURCH, GALWAY

Colin Mitchel
Died 19th Decr 178[6]
Aged 45
He was an Excelent
Actor and an
Honest Man

ST MARY'S, MOYLOUGH, CO. MEATH

May the Lord be merciful
To the soul of James Martin,
The well-known orator and antiquarian,
The philosopher, the Meath Poet,
And the unconquered controversialist
of his day. Like O'Connell, we have no one
to take his place. May he rest in peace.
Erected by his old admirer, Rev. George Leonard,
May, 1860.

Here lies the remains of
Mr. JOHN EDWIN
Of the theatre royal, who died
February twenty-two, 1803, aged thirty-three years.
His death was occasioned by the
Acuteness of his sensibility
Before he was sufficiently known to the public
Of this city to have his talents
Properly appreciated,
He experienced an illiberal and
Cruel attack on his professional reputation
FROM AN ANONYMOUS ASSASSIN.
This circumstance preyed upon his mind
To the extinction of life;
While he was in apparently bodily vigour, he
Predicted his approaching dissolution.
The consciousness of a brain rending
With agony, accounts for that
Prescience, and incontrovertibly
Establishes the cause of his death.
This stone is
Inscribed to the memory of an
Affectionate husband,
As a tribute of duty and attachment,
By her, who best acquainted with
The qualities of his heart, can best record their amiability.

GLASNEVIN CEMETERY, DUBLIN

Barry Sullivan
After life's fitful fever
He sleeps well.

ST ANN'S, DAWSON STREET, DUBLIN 2

In the Crypt
Of this church, near
The Body of her honoured Father
John Van Lewen M.D.
Lies the Mortal Part of
Mrs LAETITIA PILKINGTON
Whose Spirit hopes for
That Peace, thro' the infinite Merit of
Christ, which a cruel & merciless
World never afforded her.
Died July 29th 1750.

CABBAGE GARDEN, KEVIN STREET LOWER, DUBLIN 8

Here lies Chas Morris Makenzie
Painter
He died 13th Augt. 1808 aged 65 years
His works better
Known will speak his praise

Hunc cippum posem amicus suiss
Edvardus Hudson. R.M.D.

OLD CHURCH CEMETERY, COBH, CO. CORK

Here lie the remains of
The Rev Charles Wolfe
Late Curate of Donoughmore
Who died at Cove 21st Feb. 1823
Aged 31
The record of his genius
Piety and virtue
Lives in the hearts
Of all who knew him.
Looking unto Jesus he lived
– Looking unto Jesus he died
He is not dead but sleepeth.

Sacred to the memory
of
John Tobin Esq of Lincolns Inn
Whose remains are deposited under
The adjacent turf
He died at sea
Near the entrance of this Harbour
In the month of December
1804
On his passage to a milder climate
In search of better health
Aged 25.
That with an excellent heart
And a most amiable Disposition
He possessed a vigorous imagination
And a cultivated understanding
His dramatic writings
Evince.

BELFAST CITY CEMETERY

Sam Thompson
Playwright
1916–1965
His was the voice of many men

Erected by his friends

CHURCHTOWN GRAVEYARD, CO. CORK

Robert Oliver Reed
1938–1999
He made the air move

Reader
Whilst Science, Genius And Wit Shall Be Admired
And Merit, Charity And Worth Beloved
The Memory Of
Richard Alfred Millikin
Will Not Be Forgotten
He Died The 16th Day Of Decbr 1815
Stranger Pass On, E'en Friends May Hence Depart
Nor Gaze In Vain Nor Signs Of Grief Impart
Stranger To Self Be Timely Wise And Just
Sweet Friends Forbear Not Taunt Thy Kindred Dust
He Who Lies Here But Shares What's Due To All
He Early Knew 'Twere His To 'Bey That Call
Which Summons Man To His Eternal Rest
And Bids His Soul To Perish Or Be Blest

RATHCLAREN, COOLMAIN, CO. CORK

Tá Mé 'Mo Chodladh
Is Ná Dúisigh Mé
Doon Byrne
Born 20th Nov. 1889
Died 18th June 1928
I Am in My Sleeping
And Don't Waken Me

In the vault beneath
Are deposited the mortal remains of
Felicia Dorothea Hemans
She died May 16th 1835,
Aged 41.

Calm on the bosom of thy God,
Fair spirit, rest thee now!
Even while with us thy footstep trod,
His seal was on thy brow.
Dust. To its narrow house beneath.
Soul. To its place on high:
They that have seen thy look in death
No more may fear to die.

CASTLE ISLAND, LOUGH CARRA, CO. MAYO

George Moore
Born Moore Hall, 1852. Died 1933, London.
He forsook his family and friends for his art
But because he was faithful to his art
His family and friends
Reclaimed his ashes for Ireland.
Vale

Vale (Farewell) is one of the titles of George Moore's
three-volume autobiography.

Here lies John Flin,
To Worms akin;
Eftsoons by vagrant boys bely'd
That while he liv'd he often dy'd.
Saints oft he painted,
Himself not Sainted;
Yet leaves perhaps a fame as fair,
As many Souls of them that are.
He laugh'd at Fate,
Despis'd the great;
Was happy in his fav'rite Dram;
And pity'd those who others damn.
Liv'd to the age of sixty-seven
Spurn'd at this earth, and then flew to heav'n.

ST COLUMBA'S, DRUMCLIFFE, CO. SLIGO

Cast a cold eye
On life, on death
Horseman, pass by.

W.B. YEATS

June 1st 1865
January 28th 1939

To the Memory
Of
Captain Francis Grose
FRS
Who whilst in cheerful conversation
With friends
Expired in their arms
Without a sigh
10th of May
1791
Aged 60
Also his friend
James Gandon
Architect
Born 1743 died 1823
Captain Grose
Was a friend of Robert Burns
And the inspiration of Tam O' Shanter

Merchants, Traders, Professionals

ST MARY'S CATHEDRAL, LIMERICK

Memento Mory
Here Lieth Little Samuel Barinton,
The Great Under Taker
Of Famous City's Clock And Chime Maker;
He Made His One Time Go Early And Latter
But Now He Is Returned To God His Creator.
The 19 of November Then he Ceas'd
And For His Memory This Here Is Plac'd
By His Son Ben 1693.

FEDAMORE, CO. LIMERICK

Er by John & James Flyn,
in memr'y of their brother,
Dennis who died,
Sept 30 1807 Ag'd 27,
May he rest in peace Amen.
My sledge and hammers are declined,
my bellows too has lost the wind,
my fire extinguished,
my forge decayed,
and in the earth my vice is laid.

DUNMORE EAST, CO. WATERFORD

Here lie the remains of
John Hall, Grocer.
The world is not worth a fig,
I have good raisins for saying so.

KINNAGH, CO. WEXFORD

Here lieth the body of
Anthony Reynolds a native of
The County Tyrone
He was faithful to his employer
And, although a Miller was an honest man.
Departed this life December 13th, 1790, aged 33 years.

OLD GRAVEYARD, CORK

> Here lies Ned Stockdale, honest fellow,
> Who dy'd by fat, & lived by tallow;
> His light before men always shone,
> His mould is underneath this stone.
> Then taking things by the right handle,
> Is not this life a farthing candle?
> The longest age but a wax-taper
> A torch blown out by ev'ry vapor;
> To-day 'twill burn, to-morrow blink,
> And end as mortals in a stink.
> If this be true then worthy Ned
> Is a wax light among the dead.
> His fluted form still sheds perfume,
> And scatters lustre round his tomb:
> Then what is mortal life? Why tush,
> This mortal life's not worth a rush.

SOUTH CHAPEL, CORK

> Sargeant Malone, A Merchant from France,
> Who valued the Riches of Life
> As they secured him an interest in the next
> And in 'The Lamb's Book of Life
> Brought in Heaven a Debtor to Mercy,
> And left the balance on the Table.'

MULRANKIN GRAVEYARD, CO. WEXFORD

William Hoskins,
Dancing master,
1748
Here lyes a jolly merry blade
Who's gone;– but now he's but a shade
To teach the Ghosts a Masquerade:
But Pluto likes such a Guest
Bids him depart and go to Rest.

Collected 1752 by Bishop Pococke.
  Another source says this was a Francis Hodgenson
epitaph.

CORD CEMETERY, DROGHEDA, CO. LOUTH

Erected by
Paul O'Neil of Drogheda
To the memory
Of his brother
Bernard
An honest good
tobacco spinner
who died
1st February 1812
aged 74 years
also for him and
his posterity

CORD CEMETERY, DROGHEDA, CO. LOUTH

Erected by
Mary Clarke
22st of October 1822
in memory of
her husband
Owen Clarke
Honesty was his ambition
Industry was his amusement
And the above Mary Clarke
Died 27th July

Epitaph on an Irish chairman:

Weep, Irish lads, all true and fair men;
Here rests the leader of the chairmen.
Reader, rejoice that here lies Pat,
For was he up he'd lay you flat.
In fame, you'll never see his brother,
It reach'd from one pole to another.
And, would you know him when an angel fair,
You've nothing more to do than call, Chair! Chair!

Sacred
To the memory of Ambrose
Eaton who died March 28th
1821 agd 35 years This tomb was
erected by Five of his Brother
Tide waiters as a small mark of
Respect and Esteem for one
who possessed and daily
practised every Virtue that
rendered him an ornament
to society.

ST NICHOLAS CHURCHYARD, DUNDALK, CO. LOUTH

Erected by public subscription to the memory of
RICHARD MCKENNA
Popular native of Dundalk, for many years in the service
Of the Grand Jury of Louth, Died 3rd April 1899.
'Poor Richard, after life's fitful fever, he sleeps well.'

At the entrance to Castle Caldwell, near Lough Erne, Co. Fermanagh, there is a violin-shaped stone monument in memorial to Denis McCabe, a fiddler who fell out of a barge into the lake and drowned — and a warning to

other fiddlers against over-imbibing whiskey. The
weathered inscription from 1770 reads:

To the memory of
Denis McCabe Fiddler
who fell out of the St. Patrick Barge belonging
to Sir James Caldwell Bart. And Count of Milan,
& was drowned off this Point
August Ye 13 1770
Beware ye fidlers of ye fidlers fate
Nor tempt ye deep least ye repent too late
Ye ever have been deemed to water foes
Then shun ye lake till it with whiskey floes
On firm land only exercise your skill
There you may play and drink your fill

ST NICHOLAS CHURCHYARD, DUNDALK, CO. LOUTH

Erected by the Merchants of Dundalk in memory of
JOHN CHAMBERS
Who, during a residence among them of twenty years
Maintained the character of a sincere friend, an
Intelligent merchant, a valuable citizen and an Honest Man.
He died 7th August 1803.

As I Am, You Will Be

OLD WHITECHURCH GRAVEYARD, CO. DUBLIN

IHS
Stop
Pray as you pass by
So as you are now so once was I
As I am now so you will be
Prepare yourself and pray for me
This stone and burial ground belongs to Edward
Costello of Summerhill in
The City of Dublin May 16th 1823
Requiescant in Pace

FROM CLONDEGAD (UNKNOWN):

Here lies the body of John Glasclune
While loved and liked by all who knew him.
In his youth a chatty lad,
Lies sleeping here in Clonegad.
All you young men as you pass by,
As you are now so once was I
And as I am now so you will be,
Remember this and pray for me.

COAD CHURCH, CO. CLARE

Remember mortal who this Flag may see,
As I am now you shall hereafter be
Since Eve's Sons must nature's Tribute pay,
Soon or late must come this way.
Let true Compassion thy Kind mind dispose,
To pray for my immortal parts Repose.
This tombstone was
erected By Mr. PATRICK FOSTER
of Bankill for the use of his Father and himself and
Posterity. Use of his Father
PATRICK FOSTER who died
January the 25th 1758 age
year 73.

ST NICHOLAS CHURCHYARD, DUNDALK, CO. LOUTH

Of Barmeath once a native was
I now lie here beneath the grass
Here lieth the remains
Of Richard Jones who
Departed this transitory life
On the 17th Day of
May 1809 in the 29th year of his age
When I was young and in my prime
It pleased the Lord to end my time
Like as the Lily fresh and green
I was cut down and no more seen
You old and young, see here I lie
As you are now so once was I.

BALLINTUBBERT, CO. LAOIS

On the back of a tombstone:

> Stop stranger as you pass by,
> As you are now so once was I,
> As I am now so shall you be,
> Prepare yourself for Eternity.

> For life at best is but a crooked street,
> Death the market place where all must meet,
> If life were merchandise that gold would buy
> The rich would live
> The poor alone would die.

CRUMLIN, DUBLIN 12

> This burial ground was purchased
> by James Fitzsimons
> Of the city of Dublin Brewer
> for him and his Posterity 1783.

> Memento Mori
> Die Irae, Diea Illa
> Mortal reflect, As here I lie.
> As you are now, So once was I.
> And as I am, so must you be
> Prepare for Death, And follow me.

OLD KILCULLEN GRAVEYARD, CO. KILDARE

> Ye wiley youths, as you pass by,
> Look on my grave with weeping eye:
> Waste not your strength before it blossom
> For if you do yous will shurdley want it.

(collected by J.F. Ferguson, 1853, *Notes and Queries*)

AUGHNACLIFFE CHURCHYARD, CO. LONGFORD, 1822

> Here lies the body of John Carey.
> Remember man as you pass by
> As I am now, so will you be.
> So think on death and pray for me.

DONAGHADEE GRAVEYARD, CO. DOWN

> When on this stone you cast an eye
> Remember on mortality
> As I am now so must thou be
> Think o man that thou must die
> Here lieth ye body
> of David Hanna
> who died Febry. Ye 3 1734
> aged 24 years.

Puzzles

In the 1860s the publisher Samuel Palmer toured southern Ireland and recorded this strange epitaph. Unfortunately, he did not note its location. Perhaps it still exists?

Bene
AT. HT: HIS S. T.
Oneli ESKA
THARI Neg Rayc
Hang'd
F.R.
O! mab V. Syli Fetol
If. Ele
SS. CL.
Ayb. Ye AR
Th aN
Dcl —Ays
Hego
Therp. Elfa
ND
NO WS. HE'stur
N'D Toe ART
HH. Ersel Fy
EWEE…Pin
Gfr…I…En
D.S.L.
Et mea D

VI
Seab ATE yo
VRG
RIE Fan
DD
Ryy O! V…Rey
Esf. OR. WH.
ATA
wAi…Tsaflo
O! Doft Ears W.
Ho kNo wS.
b uT
ina RVNO
Fy Ears
In.So…Metall-
Pit…C
Hero…R…broa
D.P.
ans.He…l
N.H.
Ers Hopma
Y.B.
E.AG…AIN

For a long time Palmer and his companions were puzzled by the enigmatic inscription. Was it some kind of archaic Latin code? After re-examining the epitaph again, they noticed patterns emerging out of the cryptic text. And then the mystery was easily solved. This is what the inscription read:

> Beneath this stone lies Katharine Gray,
> Chang'd from a busy life to lifeless clay.
> By earth and clay she got her pelf.
> And now she's turn'd to earth herself.
>
> Ye weeping friends — let me advise —
> Abate your grief, and dry your eyes.
> For what awaits a flood of tears?
> Who knows, but, in a run of years,
> In some small pitcher or broad pan
> She in her shop may be again.

Can you solve this inscription on a gravestone in Ballycarry, Islandmagee, Co. Antrim? Presbyterian James Burns (1772–1864), who was a United Irishman, placed this stone on his gravesite during his life:

James Burns, Born 1772

Chr3st w1s th2 L4rd th1t sp1k2 3t,
H2 t44k th2 Br21d 1nd br1k2 3t,
1nd wh1t th1t W4rd d3d m1k2 3t,
Th1t 3 b2l32v2 1nd t1k2 3t

To solve this cryptogram it is necessary to substitute the letters A,E,I,O,U for 1,2,3,4,5 respectively and it becomes:

Christ was the Lord that spake it,
He took bread and brake it,
And what that word did make it,
That I believe and take it.

Do Not Disturb

STABANNON CHURCHYARD, CO. LOUTH

Erected by
Arthur O'Gorman, Taylor,
In memory of his Wife
Mary Cor
Who died in the 60th year of her
Age 1831. Don't open this grave
36 years after my death,
or else mark this!
(a hand holding a bludgeon)

ATHLONE ABBEY, CO. WESTMEATH

Pray for the Soul of
Denis Kelly Apothecary
Who departed this life
March 21 1849 aged 56 years
Requiescat in pace
Amen
This monument has been erected by his
Wife who earnestly requests that his grave
Shall never be disturbed.

OLD TUBRID CHURCH, CO. KILKENNY

Take heed let no one trespass
Wantonly on the remains of the dead
Old Tubrid is dedicated to God who
Had said vengeance is mine I will repay
Blessed are the dead who die in the lord
Resquiescat in pace
Erected by Thos Bowers Senr
Gragavine P.L.G. 1894

DUNCANNON FORT, CO. WEXFORD

Under Lyeth The Body Of Elizabeth
Timpson, Wife Of Captn Timpson
Who Died Ye 24th May 1736
Aged 31 Years
God Bless ye hands that lay'd this stone
And curs'd be that hands that moves her bones.

ATHLONE ABBEY, CO. WESTMEATH

It is requested that no
Person ever will intrude
On this plot of Ground
James Rutlage

Near this place is interr'd ye body of
Mr Thomas Douglas
Born in Edinburgh ye 10th of March 1630
He was endued to an eminent
Degree which ye graces of godli
ness, piety, fervent devotion un
exampled humility, benevolence
meekness & gratitude: knowing & wise in ye doctrine &
precepts of
ye Christian Religion or he strictly
practised what he knew — he lived 52 years in Stradbally
Hall,
with Alexr Dudley & Pole Cosby Esqr & was at first
employed as a preceptor
& after entertained by them for his great worth & in
gratitude for his love &
faithfulness to ye family.
He dyed ye 6th Oct of 1734 in the
Hundred & fourth year of his age
This monument was erected to his memory
By his affectit & faithl friend Pole Cosby Esq.
The sweet remembrance of the just
Shall flourish when he sleeps in dust
Psalm 112 V6.
Blest be ye men who spare his bones
And curst be they who move these stones.

CROOK, GAULTIER, CO. WATERFORD

Sacred to the memory of Anna,
wife of Lieutenant John Connor Field
of the Royal Navy and daughter of
Lieutenant David Richardson of this Parish,
who departed this life March 17th A.D. 1800
aged 18 years and 7 months.
She was a dutiful and most affectionate daughter,
a kind benevolent and tender wife.
This stone is dedicated to her memory by a husband
who adored her living and reveres her dead.
Reader,
it is hoped that as long as those virtues are respected
this stone will remain uninjured.

Animals

At the entrance to the Casino Marino, mounted on a granite plinth, is a monument to Nep (Neptune), a black Labrador, pet of the children of the second Earl of Charlemont, Francis Caulfield. Anne Bermingham, his wife, was said to have been much admired by Lord Byron and the words on the tablet are believed to have been penned by him.

Beneath, where Lillies raise their tiny crests,
All that remains of faithful Neptune rests.
Nor, stranger, scoff, if o'er his humble bier,
A Master's eye had shed affection's tear;
It is for man to scan the ways of heav'n,
And, proudly boast, to him alone, are giv'n
Those noblest emanations from above,
Truth, Honesty, Fidelity, and Love;
If such emotions in they bosom swell,
My Noble Dog possess'd them all as well,
Courage was his, in danger to defend,
Promptness to search each look, each nod attend,
Patience for hours, to brave e'en Winter's gale,
With bounding Joy, a lov'd approach to hail,
Impulsive Bound whose ev'ry action show'd
A Heart within, where fond attachment glow'd.
Faithful and True, in gentleness, a Child,
His death was placid, as his Life was mild.
Advanced in Years, in sorrow, rarely tried,
He calmly sank upon the grass and Died.

Beneath
This stone rests
VOLONEL
For 23 years the charger
And faithful friend of
Field marshal Lord Roberts
Of Khandahar
He had the honour of being decorated
By the Queen
With the Afghan medal with four clasps
The Khandahar star
And the Jubilee medal
He died at the
Royal Hospital Kilmainham June 1899

There are men both good and wise
Who hold that in a future state
Dumb creatures we have cherished
Here below
Shall give us joyous greeting when
We pass the golden gate
Is it folly that I hope it
May be so.

PORTUMNA CASTLE, CO. GALWAY

This stone is erected to the memory
Of a much lamented animal.
Who with a beauteous form possessed
Those qualities which are esteemed
Most valuable in the human species
Fidelity and gratitude.
And dying April 20th 1797 Aged 11 years
Was interred near this place.
Alas! Poor Fury
She was a dog. Take her for All in All
Eye shall not look upon her like again

POWERSCOURT HOUSE PET CEMETERY, CO. WICKLOW

EUGENIE
JERSEY COW
DIED 1967 AGED 17 YEARS
SHE HAD 17 CALVES AND PRODUCED
OVER 100,000 GALLONS OF MILK

PRINCESS
ABERDEEN ANGUS COW
DIED 1972 AGED 11 YEARS
3 TIMES DUBLIN CHAMPION

The Pride of Ballyara

Tread softly oe'r this spot
If blood can give nobility
A noble steed was he
His sire was blood
and blood his dam
and all his pedigree

This slab is in remembrance
of a famous thorough bred
that netted a fortune
for the Mullarkey Family

In Black 47 the famine yrs.
Dr. J.P. Mullarkey
Purchased 2 cargoe
of oatmeal
And 2 cargoe of potatoes
and carted to Drumartin
Aclare, Tubbercurry
as a gift.

We shall nee'r meet
his like again

POWERSCOURT HOUSE PET CEMETERY, CO. WICKLOW

DOODLES
CHOW
Died August 10th 1938
Loved and faithful friend for 14 years.
You've gone old friend
A grief too deep for tears
Fills all the emptiness
You've left behind
Gone is the dear
Companionship of years
The love that passed
All love of humankind.

**Near this spot lie buried the remains of
DICKIE BIRD, B 7.
Troop Horse 5th Dragoon Guards
Which was foaled in 1850
Joined the regiment in 1853
And served throughout the entire Crimean Campaign
From May 1854 to June 1856
He was shot on 21st Novr 1874
By special authority from the Horse Guards
To save him from being sold by auction.**

Dickie Bird was held in high esteem. Unfit army horses were sent to the knacker's yard instead of being given a formal burial, but Dickie Bird was spared this fate. In 1870 a painting of him was commissioned, and after his death his grave was marked by a wall-mounted plaque in the barracks. When cavalry horses died, it was usual to remove one of the fore-hooves as proof of death. Dickie Bird's hoof was shoed and banded with silver and attached with an engraved plaque also made of silver. It is now on display in the Royal Dragoon Guards museum in York, England.

11th (P.A.O.) Hussars
Underneath
Lies Crimean Bob
A veteran Troophorse
Who after passing unharmed
Through the memorable Crimean campaign
Died at Cahir Barracks
On the 9th November 1862
Aged 34 years.

Like Dickie Bird, Crimean Bob was spared an ignominious death and lived out his life in comfort at Cahir Barracks after surviving the horrors of the Crimean War. The original plaque is now in the Museum of the Royal Hussars in England, but a copy is on display in Cahir. Both Crimean Bob and his rider John Dyke escaped unharmed in the famous *Charge of the Light Brigade.* Dyke rose to the rank of Major, but died in 1864 at the age of 37 from tuberculosis. Ironically he lies in an unmarked grave in Glasnevin Cemetery, while Crimean Bob was buried with honours within Cahir Barracks.

POWERSCOURT HOUSE PET CEMETERY, CO. WICKLOW

STING
DIED MAY 21ST 1912
AGED 12 YEARS

FAITHFUL BEYOND HUMAN
FIDELITY

POWERSCOURT HOUSE PET CEMETERY, CO. WICKLOW

KILFANE
Irish Wolfhound
Died 20th October 1911
Universally Beloved

Long-Lived

MALAHIDE CASTLE GRAVEYARD, CO. DUBLIN

Here lies the body
Of
Peter Lamb
Departed this life
June 1789
Aged 108 years
His wife
Eliza Lamb
Departed this life
July 1791
Aged 100 years
They lived together for 80 years.

MUCKROSS ABBEY, KILLARNEY, CO. KERRY

OWEN SHINE
Who died aged 114 years
Erected
By Daniel Shine
In Memory
of his Father
Owen Shine,
Who departed
This Life April
The 6th 1847,
Aged 114 years.
Pray for him.

CASTLEBAR OLD CEMETERY, CO. MAYO

Lord have mercy on the soul of
James Faulkney
Who departed this life
April 1st 1826 aged 120 years
Also his son Anthony Faulkney
Who died 17th May 1847
Aged 90 years
Also
Bridget
His wife died December 11th 1888
Aged 80 years.

AUGHAGOWER OLD, CO. MAYO

Sacred to the memory of
Joseph Gale
Who lived to the advanced age of 137
Years without his ear being heavy or his
Eye dim. He died about the year 1770

(Various periodicals of the time state that Gale died in
February 1769 aged 129.)

ST JOHN'S CHURCH, EDGEWORTHSTOWN, CO. LONGFORD

Here Lies in hope of a blessed resurrections
The body of Andrew Burnett of Lisnaperaugh
who was born in 1710 and died in 1787
aged 77 years also the Body of Elizabeth Burnett
of Lisnageragh born 1693 married to
Andrew Burnett in 1733 died 14th September 1809
aged 116. To the last of her long life
she preserved the uses of her limbs her senses
and her memory in memory of whom this
Tomb was erected by their son John Burnett
who also departed from this life 7th June 1828 aged 85 years.

KILRANELAGH CHURCHYARD, CO. WICKLOW

**Erected by Patrick Fegan
Of Tuckmill in memory of his
Father John Fegan who depd
This life Decr 18th 1848 aged 90 yrs
Also his aunt Mary Fegan who
Departed this life Decr 1853
Aged 112 years.**

ST CANICE'S CATHEDRAL, KILKENNY

**Here lies the body of Job Whittle, who
died November 1st, 1746, aged 127 years;
Also the body of Eleanor Whittle, alias
Harrison, Wife to Joseph Whittle, who died
March 1st, 1767, Aged 65 years; likewise
the body of Joseph Whittle, son to the
above Job, and husband to Eleanor, who
departed 2nd June, 1769, aged 85 years.**

**Job, a soldier with Cromwell, this land did invade;
The patience of Job made his son Joseph reside,
Edward, Joseph's son, saw George 3rd's Jubilee;
Resigned up his soul, and leaves this to posterity.**

ST KEVIN'S CHURCHYARD, CAMDEN ROW, DUBLIN 8

**To the memory of
Henry Oliver,
aged 136 years!**

CAHERDANIEL CHURCH, DERRYNANE, CO. KERRY

A modest cross asks readers to pray

**For the soul of Rev. Patrick O'Connell,
48 years pastor of this parish. During that period,
including the Great Famine, none of his flock lost Mass
or died without the sacraments by his default.
He died May 31, 1879, in the 100th year of his age.
May he rest in peace. Amen.**

The inscription contains a mistake. Father O'Connell
was born in 1775 and died at the age of 104 years.

Erected by Thady Doorly
In memory of his son
Michael Doorly who dep
This life the 26th of Decr.
1808 aged 36 years
may he rest in peace
Amen
Also John Doorly who died
1798 aged 27 years and the
above Thaddeus Doorly who
died 1821 aged 126 years.

Here Lies

Here lies interred the treasure of our time
In vertue, with wit, and in all parts sublime,
Darby Falvey, whom God and man have blest
From his cradle to his eternal rest
He lived to the age of 68 years
And died on the 6th of March 1711.

Sir Robert Echlin, died 1757
Here lies a man without pretence,
Blessed with plain reason and common sense,
Calmly he looked on either life and here
Saw nothing to regret or there to fear.
From nature's temperate feast rose satisfied
Thanked Heaven that he lived, and that he died.

NEWTOWN GRAVEYARD, TRIM, CO. MEATH

**This monument was erected by James Potts for him
and his posterity.
Here lieth the body of his father and mother and most
affectionate...**

**All ye who roll in worldly bliss
Repent and follow me to this.**

NEWTOWN GRAVEYARD, TRIM, CO. MEATH

**Here lyeth the body of Simon Murry who departed
this life Jan 24th 1798 aged 60.
To his Maker devout,
To the poor liberal,
To mankind just.
Requ in pace.**

NEAR MOONE ABBEY, CO. KILDARE

**Under this stone lies the Body of
THOMAS ASHE Esqr. Who was
Interred here at his own Request Nine
Feet deep the 30th of June 1741 in memory
Of whom this stone and Wall was made
And Erected at the Expense of his
Three Sisters Mary Deborah and Martha**

KILKEA CASTLE CEMETERY, CO. KILDARE

Here lyeth the body
Of Robert Dixon; son
To Mr. Henry Dixon;
Of Kilkea who was
Born the 7th of July 1702
& departe this life the
10th of September 1712.

My line was short ye Long is my rest
God called me hence because he thought it Best
Believe this truth, wht wht thou valuest most
And settst thy heart upon is soonest lost.

ST JOHN'S CHURCH, FISHAMBLE STREET, DUBLIN 2

Here lies ye body of Thomas Oakes of Frances Street
Who departed if Full Assurance of Faith 1763

Sovereign Grace Redeeming Love
His theme below His song above

KILNABOY CHURCHYARD, CO. CLARE

**Under these carved and marbled Stones
Lies Terry O'Flanagan, body and bones.
Erected by his sorrowing Widow Anne O'Flannagan
1648.**

KILLACONENAGH, BEREHAVEN, CO. CORK

**Here lieth the body of Johannah Power,
Who departed this life January the 9th,
1805 aged 25 years.
Dear husband now my life is past
My life to you so long did last
Now for me no sorrow take
But love the children for my sake.**

OLD CHURCH, PORTRANE, DONABATE, CO. DUBLIN

**HERE LYETH THE
BODY OF MADAM
LYNN WHO DEPARTE[D]
THIS LIFE THE 19 DAY
OF NOVEMBER ANNO
DOMINI 1722 AGED
FORTY FIVE YEARS
OR THEREABOUTS**

KILMORE CHURCH, SUMMERHILL, CO. MEATH

**HERE LYETH YE
INGENIOUS JOHN
O'HARA WHO
DYD A.D. 1746.**

SHANAGOLDEN GRAVEYARD, SHANAGOLDEN, CO. LIMERICK

**HEARE LIES INTERRED THE BODY OF MR PEIRCE
GREEN WHO WAS KILLED BY THE TORIES
NOVEMBER THE 12 IN THE 24 YEAR OF HIS
AGE 1703.**

ANNAGH GRAVEYARD, CO. CAVAN

Beneath this stone old MICHAEL lies,
To SHERIDAN he brought no stain,
Faithful as he who in disguise,
With Charles left Culloden's plain.

Though poor was he, his mind was cast,
As his who made old Drury ring,
In humble toils his lot was cast,
His grandsire fought for Stuart's King.

FENAGH GRAVEYARD, CO. CARLOW

Here lie the remains of George Keppel late of Killane,
Who departed this life Sepr. 1st 1867 aged 36 years.
He was the loved father of Charles · Henry · James ·
Robert & Alice Keppel U.S. America.
Though ocean waves between us roll
And where our father lies
Earth has no barrier for the soul
Weel meet him in the skies.

Blessed are the pure in heart for they shall see God.
Matt. V.8.

KILMEGAN GRAVEYARD, CO. DOWN

I.H.S.
Here lieth the body of Edward Murray of Clarkhill
Who died 18th Jan 1822 aged 88 years.

Go home my friends & dry your tears,
I must lie here till Christ appears,
Repent in time whilst time you have,
There's no repentance in the grave.

THE BLUEBELL GRAVEYARD, DUBLIN 12

IHS
Here lyeth the Body of Ann Whelan
Who has not left her Fellow on the Strand
Alas she is gone that good Neighbour
Who always paid the Poor for Labour
Nor drove the Beggar from her door
But gentle was to Rich and Poor
God let her have a blessed seat
And let her Offspring all be great
The good Mother the good wife
Who done no Ill and hated Strife.

ST MARY'S COLLEGIATE CHURCH, YOUGHAL, CO. CORK

Here lies poor but honest
Cecil Pratt.
He was a most expert angler
until
death envious of his merit,
Threw out his line, and hooked him
and landed him here 14 June 1973 aged 67 years.

**Here lies the body of Edmund Spenser,
Great-Great-Great-Grandson of the Poet Spenser,
unfortunate from his cradle to his grave.**

KILCREA ABBEY, CO. CORK

**Lo; Arthur Leary, generous, handsome, brave
Slain in his bloom, lies in this humble grave
Died 4th May 1773, Aged 26 years.**

ST MARY'S COLLEGIATE CHURCH, YOUGHAL, CO. CORK

**SPE RESURGENDI:
Here lyes interr'd, his body turn'd to clay
He Liv's to Dye, he dy'd to live for aye.**

THOMAS SMYTH

**DYED YE MAY YE 21, 1669
He lov'd & Liv'd, courteous to all & kinde,
He joyed much in a contented minde;
He cared not for things heer below,
But still sayd My Redeemer lives I know.**

John Roche from Wallstown was an eccentric figure and jack-of-all-trades who built his own castle and made many ingenious devices in the eighteenth century. One of his drinking companions was a man called Nixon, who was sexton of Wallstown Church. Roche promised Nixon that he would erect a suitable headstone over his friend's grave if he survived him. In due course Nixon died and was buried in Wallstown Graveyard.

Roche kept his promise and erected a headstone over his friend's grave with the words:

HERE LIES NIXON

In the churchyard of Mayne in Clogherhead, Co. Louth, could be seen this convivial verse, until it was defaced (except the last line) around 1870.

Patrick Ward 1785

Beneath this stone here lieth one
That still his friends did please,
To Heaven, I hope, he is surely gone,
To enjoy eternal ease.

He drank, he sang while here on earth,
Lived happy as a lord
And now he hath resigned his breath,
God rest him, Paddy Ward.

DUNDALK GRAVEYARD, CO. LOUTH

Here lies the body of Robert Moore,
What signify more words?
Who Kill'd himself by eating of curds:
But if he had been ruled by Sarah his wife,
He Might have liv'd all the days of his life.

ABINGTON GRAVEYARD, CO. LIMERICK

Here lies
All that could die of
Winifred Frances Barrington
Loved and only daughter of
Sir Charles B. Barrington Bt.
Of Glenstal
And Mary Rose, his wife
Who died at Coolboreen, Co. Tipperary
15 May 1921 aged 23 years

ST PETER'S, DROGHEDA, CO. LOUTH

**Here lyeth the Body
Of Robert Smith late of
Rathmacrachan in the County of Meath Esqr. Who was
Barbarously murdered in the 70th year of his age
Together with his maid servant on the 25th of
January 1702 in the night time
By John Faulkner, Christopher Dalton, Richard Callahan,
Owen McDonnell and Patrick McDonnell
The first three of which murderers
Were executed at Trim and hanged in chains
For the said bloody and execrable fact.**

KILMALLOCK, CO. LIMERICK

Engraved on a Celtic cross in Kilmallock Churchyard is a
tribute to an unknown Fenian who died in an attack on
Kilmallock police barracks on 5 March 1867.

**Here lies one who loved his Country well
And in her sacred cause untimely fell;
Let every Irish heart who reads this scroll,
Pray God save Ireland and this martyrs soul.**

BALLYPOREEN CHURCHYARD, CO. TIPPERARY

On Teague O'Brien
Here I at length repose
My spirit now at aise is,
With the tips of my toes
And the point of my nose
Turn'd up to the roots of the daisies.

KILFANE CHURCH, CO. KILKENNY

Here lyeth deposited in hopes of
The resurrection to everlasting
Life Richard Lee late of Clay
Derla in the county of Clare
Esq. The son of Henry Lee esq
Descended from the ancient
Family of Darnold Hall in
Cheshire
He Dyed of smallpox ye
12 day of March 1707 in the
42 year of his age leaveing
only one son of 3 years old
Rarely is justice done ento the Just
In his case of necessity it must
C'Ause you'll speake well or silent be
He was composed of love and charity
A bright example to posterity
Reader if in his paths you'll rightly tread
Doubt not of being hapy when your Dead.

GREY ABBEY GRAVEYARD, CO. DOWN

Here lyes Jean Hay,
Who night and day
Was honest good and
Just her hope and love
Was from above
In which place was
her trust her spirit
left her terrane
part with joy to
God, where was her
Hart on that 4 day
Of Jany 1767.

ST MARY'S CATHEDRAL, LIMERICK

Here lies Dan Hayes
An Honest man and a
Lover of his country.

ERRIGAL—KEROGE, CO. TYRONE

Here lies the body, the soul aloft on high,
Of Nicholas McMahon, who thought in life to die;
His cares forgotten, in eternal rest
He left us here, to triumph with the blest;
73 his life, in Peter's Bark did steer,
For Heaven, in May, beneath you'll see the year,
1814.

DONAGHADEE GRAVEYARD, CO. DOWN

Here underlyeth
the body of Jean Mackgwear,
wife to Alixander
Milling of Downodie. Who lived
wel and died wel,
January 28 1660

Here lyeth the body of
Alexander Milling of this
town who departed this
life ye 9th May 1705 lived in
the fear of God and love
of his neghbors of age
73 years.